FRAMEWORK FOR CREDIT RISK MANAGEMENT

FRAMEWORK FOR CREDIT RISK MANAGEMENT

Brian Coyle

CIB PUBLISHING

BPP FINANCIAL EDUCATION

CIB Publishing
c/o The Chartered Institute of Bankers
Emmanuel House
4-9 Burgate Lane
Canterbury
Kent
CT1 2XJ
United Kingdom

Telephone: 01227 762600

CIB Publishing publications are published by The Chartered Institute of Bankers, a non-profit making registered educational charity.

Typeset by The Foundry
Printed by WBC Book Manufacturers, Bridgend

ISBN 0-85297-449-3

Contents

Introduction to Credit Risk

Credit is a concept that most businessmen understand, although it is difficult to define. Credit is both given (by the creditor) and taken (by the debtor). It represents an amount of money that will be paid at some future date, in return for benefits received earlier, such as goods purchased or loans obtained. The purpose of this book is to explain the nature of credit risk and how the risk could be managed.

What is Credit Risk?

Credit risk exists because an expected payment might not occur. Credit risk can be defined as potential losses from the refusal or inability of credit customers to pay what is owed in full and on time. Trade credit involves a supplier providing a buyer with goods or services for which payment is deferred. Bank lending involves a bank providing a loan in return for the promise of interest and capital repayment in the future. Promises to pay can be broken, withdrawn or renegotiated and altered.

Credit risk is a form of counterparty risk. Counterparty risk is the risk that the other party to a contract or agreement will fail to perform his side of the deal. This could mean a failure to provide promised goods or services, a refusal to provide promised loan facilities or a failure to pay amounts owed in full and on time.

It is more natural to think of credit risk from the point of view of the provider of credit, that may be a lending bank or a company selling goods or services on credit.

- A company that borrows from a bank might fail to repay the loan. The bank therefore has the risk of either incurring losses from a bad debt, or the potential cost of delayed payments.
- Similarly, a company that sells its goods or services on credit normally must accept the risk that the customer will fail to pay in full or that he will take longer to pay than agreed.

The definition of credit risk can be extended to include the receiver of credit. For example, there could be a risk to a buyer or borrower from the refusal or inability of suppliers and bankers, principally for financial reasons, to supply goods, services or finance that the business needs to continue operating.

Sources and Two-way Nature of Risk

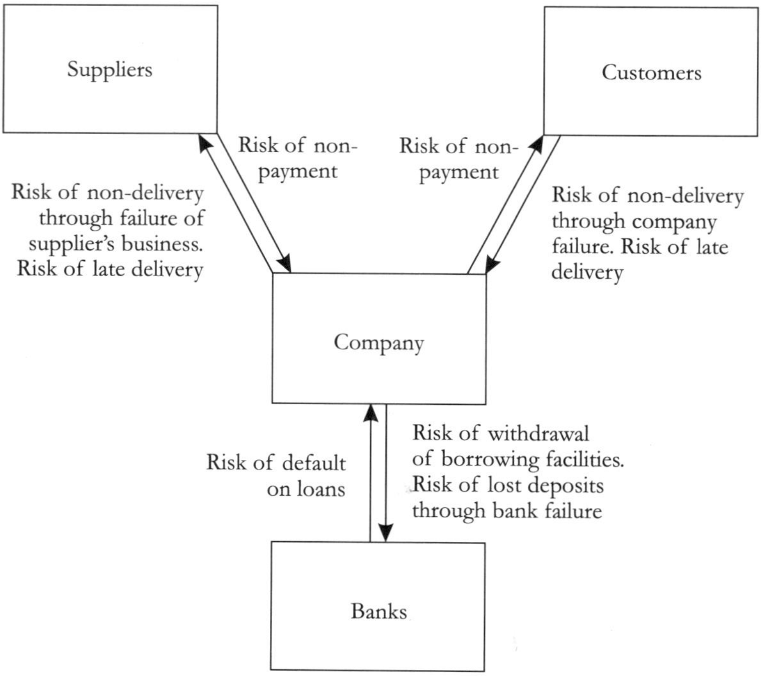

Two-way Nature of Risk

Credit risk is a two-way risk, affecting both counterparties to an agreement.

- For a supplier there could be a risk concerning the customer's ability to pay, and for the customer there could be some risk concerning the ability of the supplier to deliver.
- Similarly, a lending bank accepts some risk of the customer's inability to repay the loan. For the borrower, however, there could be a risk of the bank withdrawing its lending facilities.

The Risk-Reward Trade-Off

When a decision is taken to give credit, there has to be a trade-off between the credit risk and the reward for the lender or credit provider.

If a company grants trade credit to a customer, the risk of non-payment or late payment will depend on the situation and character of the customer. In some instances, a customer might take credit with the dishonest intent of not paying. In most instances, non-payment or slow payment is caused by

- an inability to pay on time or in full, or
- a tendency of large corporate or institutional customers deliberately to take credit from smaller suppliers beyond the due payment date, even though payment in full will be made eventually.

The risk is greater when a larger amount of credit is granted, or when credit is granted for longer periods.

The trade-off between risk and return calls for decisions about

- how much credit risk should be acceptable in order to achieve extra sales
- how much to add to the price of an order to compensate for a perceived credit risk

- what credit limits should be, both in total for the company and individually for each of the company's customers, and whether existing limits should be changed, up or down
- in some cases, whether to accept or reject a customer's order. The optimal credit decisions would maximize total returns (income) net of the costs of bad debts and delayed payments.

Example

Alpha Inc. currently expects to sell $10 million of goods each year, on which the gross profit margin is 40%. Bad debts are 1% of turnover. By offering more generous credit terms, Alpha thinks that turnover could be increased by 20%, although average debtors would be $2 million higher, and bad debts probably would increase to 5% of turnover. The cost of financing debtors is 15% per annum.

Analysis

Alpha currently expects to earn a gross profit of $4 million (40% of $10 million), with bad debts of $100,000. The change in credit policy would boost gross profit by $800,000 to $4.8 million (40% of $12 million) but bad debts would increase by $500,000 to $600,000 (5% of $12 million) and the extra financing costs would be $300,000 (15% of $2 million). There would be no net financial benefit, in this situation, from a change in credit policy.

Summary

A substantial proportion of the assets of businesses consist of trade debts. Therefore it might be useful to consider

- whether the investment in debtors is appropriate, or excessive
- whether the investment in trade debtors should be diversified to avoid the credit risk of over-reliance on particular customers or groups of customers
- how to ensure that these assets are eventually converted into cash

A balance should be achieved between risk and return. When deciding about a proposed transaction, managers should have an understanding of the credit risk involved, comparing the potential losses if the risk is realised with the potential profits from the planned transaction.

Credit risk varies according to whether the business relationship is with a customer, a bank or a supplier.

Credit Risk: Trade Credit

Trade companies can be exposed to credit risk from individuals in the form of consumers, as well as from corporate and institutional customers. The nature of the risk, and its potential consequences, are broadly the same for corporate customers and consumers, but the emphasis in this chapter is on corporate customers.

Financial Risk and Business Risk

The credit risk for a trading company arises from two sources, financial risk and business risk. Financial risk is the possibility of non-payment or late payment because of the financial circumstances, principally a lack of liquidity, of the customer.

Business risk is the possibility of a credit customer failing to pay because of circumstances connected with the customer's business activities and management. The business might suffer a setback or downturn, or management might make bad decisions, putting the company into difficulties. Management could have a deliberate policy of delaying payments to creditors for so long as possible. Late payment, as well as non-payment, is a risk for the giver of credit.

Collective Credit Risks

Although credit risk and credit assessment are more readily associated with a financial and business analysis of individual clients, they should be considered from a more global or consolidated approach also.

Credit risk will increase as a business builds up more and more debtors of a similar type. A business therefore might wish to consider its portfolio of credit customers, and the amount of credit that it should give to each identifiable group. In particular, the size of exposure to any country, any regional grouping of countries or any industry should be measured and assessed.

Customers can be grouped by country of operation or by industry.

- Country risk arises from having a number of credit customers in the same country or group of countries.
- Industry risk arises from having a number of credit customers in the same industry.

Reasons for Refusal or Inability to Pay In Full and On Time

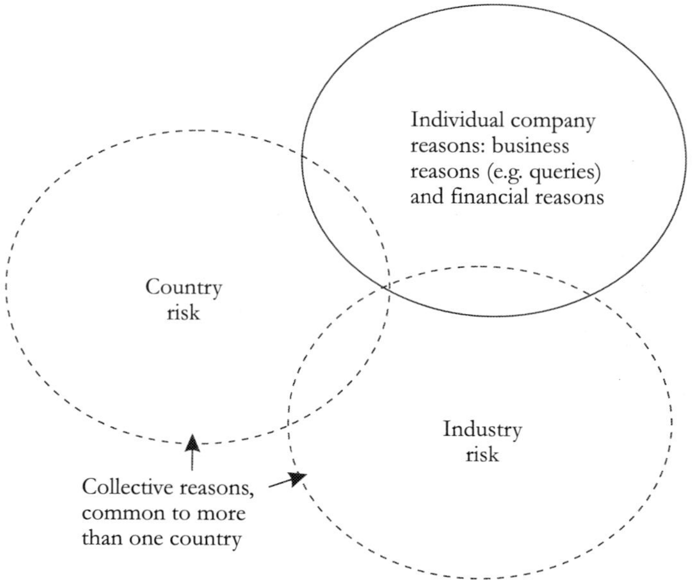

Country Risk

International companies and banks give credit to customers in a number of different countries and in a variety of different currencies. In many cases, there will be some risk in credit provision arising from factors related to that particular country.

Political risk will exist when the country's government is under political threat from within or outside its borders. A rebellion or civil war could threaten the survival of businesses in certain areas of the country, or the entire country. This has been particularly evident in the political break-up of central and eastern Europe. Occasionally, as was the case in Kuwait in 1990, a credit risk could arise from the threat of invasion, preventing business customers from paying what they owe.

Political risk is more apparent for long-term credit exposure analysis than for short-term trade credit. This is because it is easier to predict political upheaval at some time within the next two or three years than to predict change within the next few weeks or months.

Economic risk arises from economic instability, and depressed or deteriorating economic conditions within a country. Borrowers must be able to repay loans from their sources of income; trade debtors similarly must pay what they owe out of revenue from sales.

Decline in a country's economy, or in one of its particular industries, should raise questions about whether to grant credit to customers in that country, and if so, whether to limit the amount of credit. The Asian crisis has meant that both companies (trade debts) and banks (bank loans) have had to revise their policies towards counterparties.

Currency risk exists with any cross-border lending, because of the volatility of foreign exchange rates.

- For a US company giving credit abroad in a foreign currency, there is a risk that the currency of the debt will decline in value during the credit period. Unless this exposure to a worsening exchange rate is hedged (perhaps through forward exchange contracts), the value of the debt will decline over time.

- For a US company or organisation giving credit abroad in dollars there is a risk that an increase in the foreign exchange value of dollars could result in bad debts by squeezing the profit margins of overseas borrowers.

For major multinational companies and international banks, their total unhedged exposures to currency risk through lending or granting trade credit should be kept within a tightly managed limit.

The legal system in a particular country could be a credit risk, particularly to smaller companies without the money or resources to pursue recalcitrant debtors through the law courts of that country. Customers might try to use the legal system in their own country to delay or to avoid having to pay money. A case in point, and well publicized at the time, was the difficulty experienced by the administrators of Polly Peck International during 1990/91 in tracing what had happened to cash of the group within northern Cyprus. Their efforts were stalled by legal procedures in the Cypriot courts.

National culture occasionally can create some credit risk within a particular country. For example, in some countries there is an acceptance that debts can be paid late and only after persistent demands from the supplier. Customers who pay late are simply conforming to what is normally expected, and would not see themselves as behaving badly.

Industry Risk

Credit exposure to a number of customers in a particular industry also can be a serious credit risk, and companies should consider whether this exposure could be controlled.

The risks of industry exposure are likely to be greatest when the domestic or international economy is suffering from a downturn or recession, when some industries, such as construction and chemicals, often appear to suffer earlier and more severely from adverse economic conditions. For example, the economic recession in the early 1990s was preceded by a severe downturn in the property industry. Falling property values and falling demand for property hit the income and net worth of property companies, many of which collapsed as a result. Banks, with loans to property companies secured on assets whose value had tumbled, incurred losses from their credit exposure to the property industry.

Occasionally, an industry might undergo a long-term structural change within a relatively short period of time. Technological change could cause an industry to decline severely or even collapse. Better quality and/or lower-priced imports might appear on the market, and could undermine a domestic industry.

Many companies are involved in a supply chain (value chain) within a particular industry, and credit therefore must be given almost entirely to customers in just that one industry. Producers of steel, for example, are heavily exposed to industries using steel as a raw material, such as car manufacturers. Similarly, food producers are heavily exposed to the retail industry, large supermarket chains in particular.

Value Chain

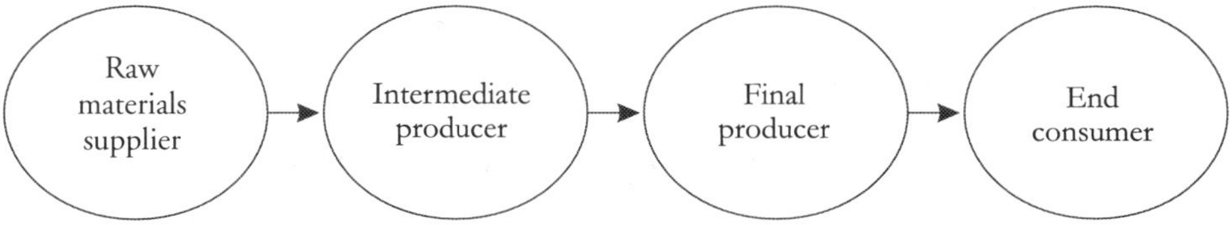

The supply chain is significant for credit management for two reasons.

- A customer who produces at an early stage in the supply chain is vulnerable to an economic downturn in the market for the end product. Falling car sales, for example, will hit manufacturers of steel gearboxes and tires as badly as the car producers themselves. Similarly, an announcement that Nissan at some stage would make catalytic converters with a cheaper metal hit the market price of platinum, the material then used for their manufacture.
- A producer with all its customers in a particular industry cannot avoid credit exposure to that industry. Tire producers cannot avoid credit exposures to the vehicle manufacturing industry. Similarly, an airplane producer cannot avoid credit exposure to airlines for

civilian airplanes or to governments for military airplanes except by arranging credit insurance to obtain protection against many such credit risks.

If it is difficult for a company to restrict its credit exposures to any particular industry, it still should be possible to control credit

- in total
- to any particular country, especially one that might have a high-risk credit rating
- to any particular customer.

Individual Customers and Credit Risk

Any company that relies heavily on just one customer for most of its business will be commercially vulnerable. Credit exposures to that customer will be overshadowed by the even greater strategic business risk, namely the danger that the customer will take his business elsewhere or might run into trading difficulties and reduce the volume of orders.

The amount of credit granted to any individual customer should be kept under control. Management should be aware of the amount of credit it can afford to give, and the potential consequences of over-exposure to any single customer. For example, suppose that a company has an annual turnover of $24 million, 50% of which comes from a single customer, with sales volume spread fairly evenly throughout the year. If this customer had been in the habit of paying its invoices after 30 days and then starts to delay payment until 60 days after invoice, there will be a 30-day gap in the payment stream, during which the supplier company will have to forego a cash inflow of about $1 million.

The supplier obviously will try to persuade the customer to revert to paying after 30 days, but when the customer is so important to the supplier's business, it might not be possible to do this. If the supplier could not finance a loss of $1 million in cash inflows in any month, arising from the customer's decision to delay payments from 30 to 60 days, the fault arguably would be with the supplier's management for allowing the company to become so over-exposed to credit risk in the first place.

The Potential Cost of Exposures

The potential cost of a credit risk exposure to a customer is the loss that would be incurred if the debt were unpaid or if payment were delayed.

There is an interest cost for late payment. This is either the bank overdraft cost of financing the debt beyond the due payment date, or the interest income foregone. For example, if a company has a bank overdraft with interest at 14% per annum, the cost of delayed payment on a debt of $10,000 would be $3.84 for each day of the payment delay. If a company has debtors of $10 million who postpone payment beyond the due date, the interest cost would be over $3,800 per day of delay.

The cost of a bad debt can be measured in at least three ways. Suppose that goods are sold on credit to a customer for $10,000. The cost of the goods consisted of $4,000 in cash items of expenditure plus $3,000 of overheads. If the customer fails to pay, the cost of the bad debt could be stated as

- $10,000, the revenue not received
- $7,000, the cost of the goods sold, or
- $4,000, the cash expenditures incurred in making the sale.

During the period of credit exposure, the most accurate measurement of the potential cost of the credit risk is the cash income that is expected, but which will not be earned if the debt proves bad. In this example, the potential cost of the credit risk from a bad debt is probably best stated as $10,000.

The risk of bad debts and late payments also could create a liquidity risk for a company that has insufficient cash or borrowing capability to finance an excessive burden of debtors. Credit risk therefore could result in insolvency, not just lost income or reduced profits.

The total credit given by a company to its customers is a function of

- the amount of each credit transaction
- the volume of credit transactions, and
- the length of the credit period.

Exposures to credit risk begin with the creation of the debt, and end with payment from the customer. They can be measured by the total volume of debtors, and analyzed according to the length of credit given. Restricting the total volume of debtors, partly perhaps by limiting the credit period, can contain the risk.

Credit Risk and Other Financial Risks

Credit risk in a transaction can exist in tandem with another financial risk, such as currency risk or interest-rate risk.

Example 1
Beta Inc. sells goods to an overseas customer at a price of $180,000, payable in two months. Beta decides to hedge the currency risk by arranging a forward contract to sell at a rate of $2 = £1. The customer fails to pay the $180,000 after two months, and Beta's credit risk exposure turns into a bad debt.

Analysis
Beta would have to honor its forward contract to sell $180,000 at $2 = £1 by purchasing dollars at the spot rate. If the dollar had strengthened in the two-month credit period, say to $1.80 = £1, there would be a loss on the currency dealings, adding to the credit risk loss.

Example 2
Gamma has entered into a three-year interest rate swap agreement with Omega Bank. The notional principal is $20 million. Under the terms of the swap agreement, exchanges of interest payments take place every six

months. Gamma pays Omega Bank a fixed rate of 10% per annum, and in return Omega Bank pays Gamma the six-month LIBOR rate.

At the end of the first six-month period, six-month LIBOR is 9% per annum, and Gamma therefore must make a net payment to Omega Bank of $100,000 ($20 million x 6/12 x (10% - 9%)). Gamma fails to make this payment.

Analysis
Gamma owes money to Omega Bank under the terms of the swap agreement because variable interest rates are below the fixed swap rate of 10%. An interest rate exposure has crystallized for Gamma, and Gamma owes $100,000. Omega Bank now has a credit risk exposure to Gamma because it is owed this amount. Gamma's failure to pay the money due to Omega Bank means that the bank has suffered a loss from its credit exposure to Gamma.

Risk and the Supplier

Companies sometimes can be put at risk by the financial instability of a major supplier. If a supplier were to go out of business, the company would have to find an alternative source of supply, possibly having to pay a higher price or accept stricter credit terms from a new supplier. Suppliers with cash flow problems might try to ask for earlier payment than in the past. In some cases, a customer might feel obliged to make payments with its order, simply to help keep the supplier in business.

The risk from financially weak suppliers can be regarded as a credit risk in the sense that credit arrangements might be lost or become more restricted. As part of its credit risk management planning, a company should consider the sourcing of raw materials, services and fixed assets, and carry out checks on the financial strength of its major suppliers.

Many companies now employ a just-in-time purchasing system that was originally pioneered by the Japanese car manufacturing industry. In practice, this means that a company will hold only enough stock to meet immediate demand. To work properly, such a system relies on the ability of major suppliers to deliver the goods or services on time and to the specified quality standard. Companies employing the JIT system could be heavily exposed to the financial weakness of a key supplier. The system also needs to be supported by an efficient electronic data interchange (EDI) system, where documents such as orders or invoices are exchanged in electronic form.

Credit Risk: Bank Credit

Credit risk exists in lending transactions between banks and their customers, for both the borrower and the lender.

Risk for the Bank

The credit risk for a lending bank is readily apparent. The customer might be unable to pay interest on a loan, or to repay the loan principal. The bad debt problems of Japanese banks in the mid to late nineties, for example, were widely reported. Injudicious lending to the property sector in Japan coupled with lending to customers in the economies of southeast Asia resulted in severe problems during the period 1997/98. Many borrowers were unable to repay loans, and lending banks had to make substantial provisions and/or write-offs.

A bank loan can have three sources for repayment

- the cash flows of the borrower
- security, in the form of a fixed or floating charge on the borrower's assets, or a mortgage on property
- a guarantee from a third party, such as a holding company.

Lending banks commonly look for at least two of these sources of repayment for any loan that they make. In the case of corporate borrowers, banks will expect loans to be repaid normally out of the operational cash flows of the company. The bank will try to obtain some assurance or comfort that the borrower to whom the bank will be exposed for credit risk will have the liquidity to repay the loan. Taking security such as a charge on assets of the borrower, is a fallback source of repayment. In the event that the company is unable to generate enough cash to service a secured loan, the bank can, if it chooses, call in the loan and seek repayment from the sale of the secured assets. In the case of a guaranteed loan, the bank would ask the guarantor for payment.

However, as past experience has shown, banks can be inadequately protected against credit risk, even when loans are secured. This can happen when the value of the secured assets falls below the amount of the loan. A collapse in the property market, for example, would increase the credit risk of banks lending to property and building companies. Another effect would be to decrease the value of any property that had been taken to secure bank loans.

Example
Omega Bank made a loan of $2 million to Alpha Inc., secured against commercial property owned by Alpha with a market value of $2.5 million. Subsequently, a decline in business left Alpha unable to repay the loan.

Credit Risk and Secured Loans

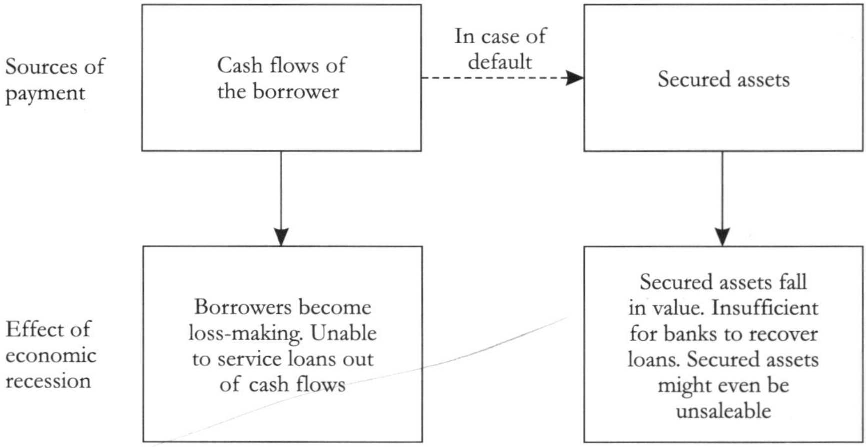

Analysis
Omega Bank could decide to call in its security and sell the commercial property to obtain repayment of the loan. If there had been a collapse in the property market the property might be no longer worth $2 million, and could even have no ready buyer except at a very low price. Omega Bank would be unable to avoid a bad debt.

Restricting Bad Debts

There are various ways of trying to keep bad debts on loans to a tolerable, low level, including

- avoiding loans to risky customers
- monitoring loan repayments, and
- renegotiating loans when customers get into difficulties.

Loans should be made only to borrowers who are likely to be able to repay, and who are unlikely to become insolvent. Credit analysis of potential borrowers is carried out in order to judge the credit risk with the borrower and to reach a lending decision. Loan payments are monitored, and action taken whenever a customer defaults, for example, by failing to make a payment of interest on the due date. The bank should be in a position to discuss the problem with the customer as soon as it becomes apparent. Where necessary, the loan can be called in.

A bank could agree to support a borrower who is unable to meet its loan repayment schedule. The conditions of the loan can be altered; for example, loan covenants can be made less restrictive. Alternatively, the borrower could be allowed an interest holiday, or the term of the loan could be extended. In some cases, a bank might agree to a refinancing package in which the borrower is given enough new loans to pay off maturing loans with interest.

The extent of bank support for borrowers in difficulties can be extensive, particularly during a recession. Banks might hope that with eventual economic recovery, customers' businesses would improve and allow them to pay off their loans. The banks would then have succeeded both in avoiding bad debt write-offs and in maintaining their customer base for the future. A second reason for supporting borrowers in difficulties, particularly during a recession, is that banks would otherwise have to write off even more loans as bad debts, and so report even lower profits (or bigger losses) themselves.

The difficulty for banks in supporting hospital cases is that their credit exposure to the borrower increases. There is the risk that if the borrower eventually goes out of business, the bad debt for the bank will be even higher than if it had called in its loans earlier.

Example
Alpha borrowed $5 million from Epsilon Bank at an interest rate of 14%, with interest payable quarterly. Because of a downturn in its business, Alpha is unable to make an interest payment, and Epsilon Bank agrees to roll up the unpaid interest into the loan.

Analysis
Alpha is a bad debt risk, but Epsilon Bank has decided to support Alpha, in effect by giving a three-month interest holiday. Alpha's loan has increased from $5 million to $5.175 million, because unpaid interest of $175,000 has been added to the loan.

Epsilon Bank can report a profit of $175,000 on its loan transaction with Alpha that is the interest earned but added to the loan. The bank has received no cash income from Alpha, however, and its credit risk exposure is $175,000 higher.

Credit Risk and Interest Rates

Banks can protect themselves against credit risk to some extent by increasing the interest cost on loans to borrowers. The income from good borrowers can then offset bad debt losses.

Example
Center Bank has a loan portfolio of $100 million, on which it is seeking annual interest income of $10 million net of bad debt write-offs.

Analysis
If the bank expects no bad debts, it could charge interest of 10% on its loans, to earn annual income of $10 million. But because of bad debts the interest rate on performing loans would have to be increased, as shown:

	Bad debts	**Performing loans**	**Net income required**	**Interest income required**	**Interest rate**
	(1)		(2)	(1) + (2)	
%	$m	$m	$m	$m	%
0	0	100	10	10	(10 ÷ 100) 10.0
1	1	99	10	11	(11 ÷ 99) 11.1
2	2	98	10	12	(12 ÷ 98) 12.2
5	5	95	10	15	(15 ÷ 95) 15.8
10	10	90	10	20	(20 ÷ 90) 22.2

To the extent that banks raise interest rates as protection against credit risk, the cost of borrowing to other customers is higher.

Risks for the Customer

There is some credit risk for customers in their dealings with a bank. In exceptional circumstances, such as the collapse of the Bank of Credit and Commerce International (BCCI) and Barings, customer deposits are at risk to the financial collapse of the bank.

More commonly, borrowers are at some risk from the lending decisions of their banks. The risk arises from taking credit rather than from giving it. The borrower's risks can be listed briefly.

- The interest rate charged by the bank will be dependent on the bank's view of the borrower's creditworthiness.
- A bank might decide to reduce a customer's borrowing facility.

By reducing an overdraft facility, a bank could force a company into liquidation.

- Lending covenants on an existing loan could restrict the ability of the borrower to obtain further loans.
- A bank might refuse to extend a loan to support a company with temporary cash flow difficulties, caused perhaps by a delay in payment on a major contract, or a delayed start to a major project.

Borrowers could reduce these borrowing risks by ensuring that they are able to make interest payments and repay loans on schedule. However, given the uncertainties of business, companies could find themselves in need of larger borrowings or an extension to the term of their loans. The risk could be controlled, perhaps in the choice of lending banks by the borrower, and in the development of a good relationship between customer and bank.

Summary

Credit risk management calls for controls over the taking of credit, as well as the giving of credit. This is the case for trade credit and borrowing.

How companies, including banks, can establish and operate a system for credit management planning and control will be considered in the following chapters.

Elements of Credit Management

Credit management is concerned primarily with managing debtors and financing debts. The objectives of credit management can be stated as safeguarding the company's investment in debtors and optimizing operational cash flows. Policies and procedures must be applied for granting credit to customers, collecting payment and limiting the risks of non-payment.

The objectives of credit management are achieved primarily by means of a health monitoring function, i.e.

- assessing the credit risks and other risks, such as currency risks
- negotiating and arranging credit terms appropriate to those risks
- collecting payments in accordance with the agreed terms.

Credit Control

An important function of credit management is credit control. This is primarily a process of deciding how much credit should be given to customers or borrowers, and ensuring compliance with the credit terms that are set. Controlling credit is necessary

- to avoid a liquidity shortage from excessive investment in debtors or loans, and
- to secure an optimum balance between giving credit to make more sales and the financial risks from non-payment or late payment.

Poor credit control heightens the risks to liquidity and profitability.

Elements of Credit Management

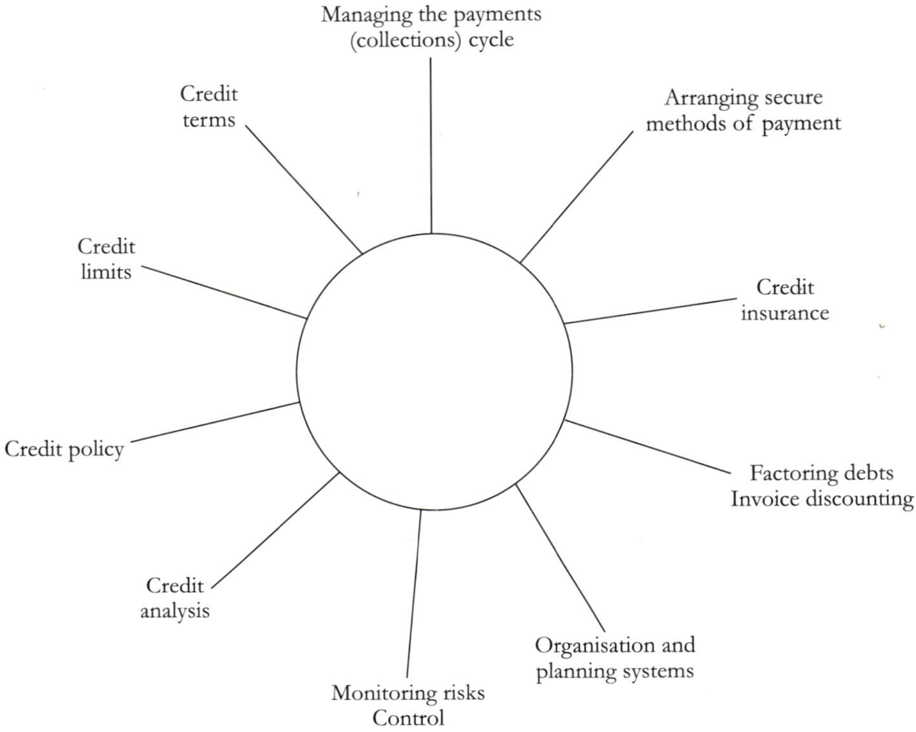

A credit control system should include procedures for deciding how much credit to take, as well as how much to give. Risks can arise from over-exposure to a particular bank (for loans obtained) or to a particular supplier (for trade credit received).

The Importance of Credit Control

Granting trade credit is an important aspect of business activity in many companies. It is usual for a company's debtors, particularly in service industries, to make up a large proportion of its total assets. For a company with total assets, including equipment, motor vehicles, stocks, debtors, etc., of $10 million, debtors typically could make up $2-3 million of the total.

The control of debtors can be a significant factor in a company's financial performance. An important measure of company profitability is its return on assets employed. This is the profit expressed as a percentage of the value of the company's assets. If debtors are not well managed, there could be several financial consequences.

- The amount of unpaid debts will be high, and there will be more debtors than there should be.
- Excessive debtors add to the cost of the assets employed by the company, and this will reduce the percentage return on assets.
- Debtors represent unpaid invoices that have to be financed by the company, and this creates an interest cost for the company.
- The risk of bad debts will be greater. Bad debts have a direct effect on profits.

Example

Alpha Inc. has total assets of $6 million including debtors of $1.5 million. Annual sales are $10 million. The company has a bank overdraft that could be reduced if debtors paid more promptly, but that will rise if the total amount of unpaid debts increases. Interest on the overdraft is 10% per annum.

Suppose that because of poor credit management Alpha's debtors increase by half a million dollars to $2 million, and bad debts rise by 0.75% of sales turnover.

Analysis

Alpha's poor credit management will affect its financial performance as follows.

- Annual profits fall by $75,000 (0.75% of $10 million) because of the higher bad debt risk.
- The increase in debtors has to be financed (because the company has to wait longer to recover the money it has spent on making the sales). The annual interest cost of the rise in debtors by $500,000 could be about $50,000 (10% of $500,000).

- Lower profits and higher assets, i.e. more debtors, will result in a fall in the company's return on assets employed.

Efficient credit management therefore should limit both the cost of bad debts and the interest cost of allowing excessive credit.

Achieving Credit Control

Credit control is a continual process consisting of the following elements

- establishing principles to apply in lending decisions or decisions about granting credit
- formulating and implementing a policy for credit; for example, deciding normal credit terms to customers and setting maximum credit limits for the company's debtors in total
- credit assessment of individual customers, for decisions about whether to grant credit to them
- operational management of the credit cycle, i.e. invoicing and collection procedures and query control
- monitoring the creditworthiness and credit limits of customers
- arranging secure methods of payment, where normal credit terms cannot be offered without unacceptable risk
- continual monitoring of debtors and bad debts against policy and other targets
- establishing and maintaining an organization for credit control.

These activities occur with differing regularity and frequency, although it might be useful to depict them as a sequence of events, as shown in the diagram opposite. The chapters that follow will discuss each of these activities in turn.

Credit Control Activities

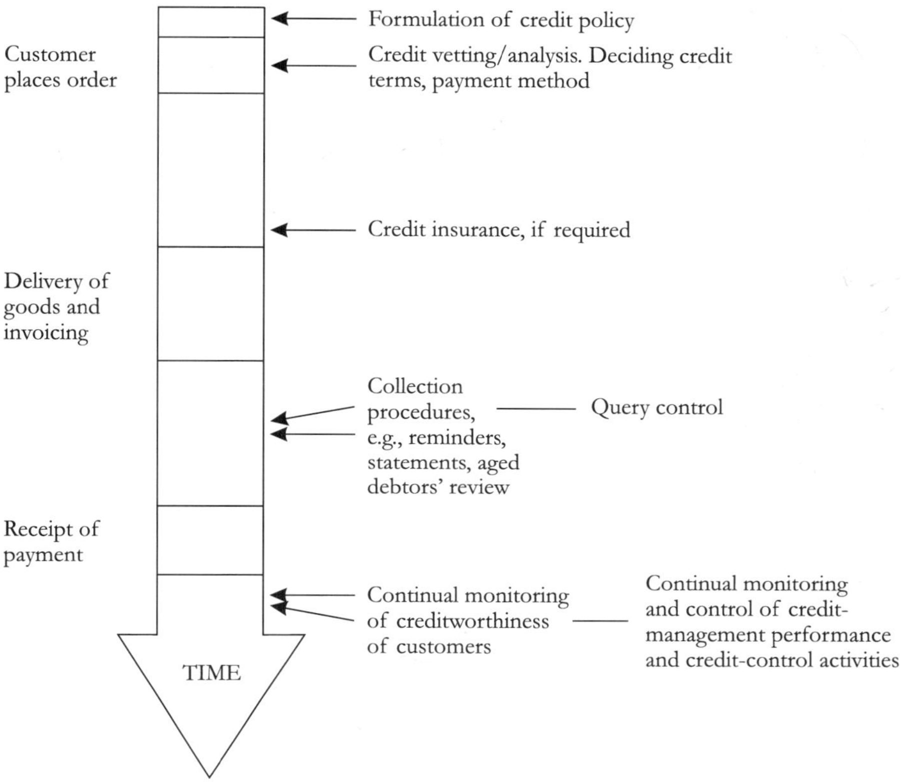

Credit Control as an Element of Marketing

Credit control is an element of the marketing mix, as part of the customer service function. The credit department could have regular contact with customers, and the service that it provides could help shape a customer's perceptions of the company.

The handling of requests for credit and establishing credit terms should be part of the selling service. If a client isn't given as much credit as required, the method of refusal could affect future business relationships with the company. Credit needs to be controlled, but also should be comparable with credit terms offered by competitors. A recent study carried out by a credit management research group found that companies that took the trouble to check out customers before starting to do business with them – checking ability to pay, negotiating terms, checking orders against creditworthiness – had a greater proportion of sales paid on time and bad debts were 84% lower.

Queries and complaint procedures also should be efficient, to satisfy customers and at the same time to speed up payments that are delayed while the queries are processed.

Credit can be a feature of price. A price of $10,000 cash with order is just as expensive as a price of $10,300 when the customer is given three months' credit and interest rates are 12% per annum, because the credit period gives the customer an interest benefit of $300 ($10,000 x 12% x 3/12).

Influences on Credit Management

Several developments have influenced credit management including

- high interest rates
- availability of bank loans
- low profits and cash flow problems
- growing use of computer systems.

High Interest Rates

High interest rates generally are a feature of an economic recession, where they are adopted as a favored policy to control inflation. They also affect the cost of granting credit. Companies should recognize the cost of credit, and make credit decisions with this in mind. An awareness of the cost should be communicated to credit managers, for example by means of a regular memo stating what current credit terms are costing the company.

Example

Beta Inc.'s finance director is concerned about the finance cost of granting credit. The cost of borrowing for the company currently is 12% per annum (1% per month).

Analysis

A memo could be sent by the finance director to credit controllers and sales staff, indicating that the current cost of credit is $10 per month for every $1,000 of credit given ($1,000 x 12% ÷ 12 months).

Suppose that a salesman is negotiating credit terms with a customer for a $20,000 sale that should yield a gross profit of $6,000. The customer has asked for 90 days' credit; normal company policy is to offer 30 days' net. The salesman would be able to calculate that, by agreeing to the customer's request, the cost of credit would be $600 ($20,000 x $10 per 1,000 per month x three months), rather than $200 ($20,000 x $10 per 1,000 per month x 1 month) if normal credit terms were applied. This would reduce the expected profit on the sale from $5,800 ($6,000-$200) to $5,400 ($6,000-$44600), a reduction of about seven per cent.

Availability of Bank Loans

The availability of bank credit is dependent on the current capital adequacy rules and the state of the economy, insofar as to what extent the bank has suffered bad debt losses. In times of a credit squeeze, most small companies are vulnerable because they often rely on bank loans to finance their business. And unlike most large companies, they do not have ready access to alternative sources of loan finance, such as bonds or commercial paper.

The reluctance of banks to lend could force companies to rely more heavily on trade credit. However, suppliers have become much more conscious of credit risk as a result of past recessions, and many are now much more wary about granting credit.

Low Profitability and Poor Cash Flows

The cost of granting credit can be particularly severe for companies with low profits and cash flow problems. During times of economic recession, the average time taken by customers to pay their trade debts usually increases substantially.

Customers can delay payments to ease their cash flow difficulties, but in doing so, they could be passing on similar difficulties to the supplier.

A review of examples of actual cash flow problems quoted a small businessman explaining why his company had collapsed: "It was mainly bad debts. The banks tell you to do a credit check on your customers but that doesn't mean a thing. Sometimes even your big customers go down while others tell you they are not satisfied with the work you have done and hold back payment."

In a recession these problems can be particularly severe for small companies that often have a smaller customer base than those of larger companies. Even so, credit risk can threaten the financial stability of any size of business.

Computerized Credit Information

There has been a gradual increase in the use of computers for credit management. Credit reference agencies maintain a database about businesses, and most large agencies can transmit credit information electronically to clients.

Companies also can use their own computerized sales ledger systems to provide credit management reports; for example, a regular aged debtors analysis, listing overdue debts.

Poor payment problems also can be reduced by ensuring clarity of invoices. In March 1998, a proposal for a European Parliament and Council Directive combating late payment in commercial transactions, was put before the European Parliament for its opinion.

Credit Management in Banks and Other Companies

It can be tempting to assume that credit management in banks is very different from credit management in other companies. In spite of differences in organization and management responsibilities, banks and other companies face similar credit management issues.

All organizations should have a policy for credit. For banks, granting credit is their business, and a policy framework is essential. Non-bank companies, however, should formulate a policy for credit, to ensure that credit risk does not threaten the financial stability of the company.

Individual applications for credit have to be vetted. Banks handle applications regularly, and have established routine procedures and systems. Other companies normally handle credit applications much less frequently than banks, but a vetting and assessment system should exist. Credit analysis methods are similar for all types of company, including banks. Banks have the staff expertise, however, to rely mainly on in-house credit assessments, whereas smaller companies could rely on external sources of credit information, such as credit-reference agencies.

Customer accounts should be monitored. Suppliers will monitor the payment records of each customer while banks will review the performance of the customer's account.

However, there are some differences in the way banks and other companies manage credit. Trade suppliers must establish procedures for invoicing, collecting payments and chasing non-payers. Banks often are in a position to debit a customer's current account, to ensure prompt payment. Chasing non-payment is necessary only if the customer has an account with another bank, or when the balance on the customer's account is insufficient.

There are also differences in the approach of banks and suppliers to security of payment. Banks can ask for security in the form of a fixed or floating charge over the customer's assets, or in the form of a third party guarantee. When the risk is judged high in spite of the security, a bank also has the option of charging a higher interest rate.

Trade suppliers must try to obtain security of payment, should they require it, by different methods, such as retention of title clauses, letters of credit, credit insurance and factoring.

In spite of the differences, however, it is important to recognize that credit management, particularly the processes of setting policy, credit assessments and credit monitoring, is essentially the same for both financial and non-financial organizations.

Summary

Credit control is both a finance and a marketing activity. From a financial point of view, credit control is needed to monitor and limit credit risk, and to manage a company's debtors. In marketing, it provides an important point of contact between a company and its customers. Credit policy and procedures should try to ensure that a workable and suitable balance is struck between the need to generate sales and the need to control financial risk.

Companies and banks should have a system in place for assessing and controlling credit risk. Guidelines for credit management are suggested in the table opposite.

Guidelines for a Credit Management Policy

Credit Policy

- Establish a credit policy for determining how much credit to give, and on what terms
- Set out a clear policy for dealing with late payers, including a policy on taking non-payers to court.

Credit Vetting

- Take credit references on all new customers, or carry out credit analysis in-house
- Update credit references and credit ratings regularly
- Do not allow individual customers to take more credit than the company would be able to afford if the customer were to become a bad debt
- Apply the principles of good lending to requests from customers for credit.

Collection Procedures and Credit Monitoring

- Establish efficient procedures for collections and query control
- Monitor customer-payment records and review credit terms
- Chase up late payers promptly.

Security of Payment

- Where appropriate, ask for personal guarantees from the customer
- If suitable, take out credit insurance
- If negotiable, arrange for payment or part-payment in advance, e.g. against shipment.

Principles of Good Lending

When assessing lending proposals banks apply certain general principles of good lending, often referred to as the canons of lending. Although not all of these principles can be applied by corporate credit managers to requests for trade credit, most are generally applicable. They provide an excellent framework for assessing all credit proposals.

Because the purpose of lending is to earn interest and make a profit, it follows that these principles of good lending should be concerned with ensuring, so far as possible, that the borrower will be able to make the scheduled repayments with interest, in full and within the required time period. Otherwise, the profit from any interest earned is reduced or even wiped out by the bad debt when the customer eventually defaults.

The Lending Proposition

The initial lending/borrowing proposition must come from the customer. The customer must ask to borrow a certain amount of money for a certain period of time and for a particular purpose, making it clear how the bank can expect to be repaid. It is then the task of the banker to decide whether the proposition is acceptable in its current form, whether it would be acceptable if it were amended, or whether it is not acceptable in any form.

If a bank agrees to lend, it will want to structure the loan or facility to match the purpose for which it is being given.

Analyzing Lending Propositions

Many lending decisions are based on experience and on the banker's instinct that the customer will repay the loan promptly and in full. However, a structured objective approach should be used. One such approach is to consider each important factor in turn and assess whether the lending proposition satisfies certain criteria.

The banks' principles of good lending to corporate customers can be reduced to a simplified framework, CAMPARI and ICE.

The mnemonic CAMPARI and ICE stands for issues relevant to the lending proposition:

C Character
A Ability
M Means
P Purpose
A Amount
R Repayment
I Insurance

and

I Interest
C Commissions
E Extras

Character

The character of the borrower always will be a prime factor in any lending decision. Banks are often willing to lend on the assurance of a particular person, management team or company name, although if taken to an extreme, a name-lending policy can be dangerous and may result in bad debts. A lender must be wary of a borrower who could commit fraud.

Integrity and honesty are not the only aspects of character to consider, however. Honest customers are not necessarily creditworthy. It is usually more important to assess character in terms of whether

- the owners or directors have a financial interest in the business
- the departmental management is of good caliber
- the business premises give the impression of a well-run unit
- the company has well-regarded financial advisers and if so, how established the relationship is between the company and those financial advisers.

The character of the borrower can be judged by either or both of these two methods

- *Past record* A banker can look at the history of the customer's account with the bank to establish whether he or she has kept good control over his or her money in the past. If the borrower does not have an account with the bank, the banker should pay particular attention to why the company has decided against asking its own bank for the advance.
- *Personal interview* The customer's character can be assessed from a personal meeting, preferably reinforced by a visit to the customer's premises. However, it is not good enough for a banker to conclude, on the basis of an interview and personal impression, that the borrower is of good character or strong ability. There ought to be factual information on which to assess the customer's qualities in these respects.

Ability

Ability here is meant not in the context of whether the customer has the ability to repay, but relates to whether the borrower has the ability to enter into a contract with the bank to borrow.

For example, when a company wishing to borrow is part of a larger group, it is essential to identify its status within the group, in order to assess the potential credit risk for the lender. A group of companies is not necessarily a legal entity. When one company in a group borrows money, the bank's transaction is not with the group as a whole. In the event of default and non-payment of loan interest or principal, the lender cannot take action against the entire group, nor the parent company, only the company that has borrowed.

Therefore a lender must be satisfied with the creditworthiness of the borrowing company, and can rely on the collective financial strength of the group only in cases where

- the borrowing company is the parent company of the group, or
- the parent company and/or other companies in the group provides a guarantee of payment to the lender, in the event that the borrowing company fails to honor its payment obligations.

A parent company could, for example, create a subsidiary company specifically for the purpose of borrowing or carrying out other specific financial transactions on behalf of the rest of the group. In such cases, a lender would have a credit exposure to this company only, and would not have a claim on any of the group's assets in the event of default by the borrowing subsidiary. Even when the subsidiary is part of a major group whose debt capital has a triple-A credit rating, a lender will have a high credit risk exposure if it lends to a subsidiary that is financially weak.

A lender should refuse a loan to a subsidiary company unless the subsidiary is financially strong, or unless other companies in the group are willing to provide guarantees.

As a general rule, when a bank lends to one subsidiary in a group, the parent company will not allow the subsidiary to default on its payment obligations. However, cases have arisen where a group has used one subsidiary for all its borrowings, and then allowed it to go into liquidation with unpaid debts, leaving all the other companies in the group intact and debt free.

When lending to a company, the bank should also ascertain whether the directors are acting within the authority extended to them in the company's articles of incorporation. A comparison also can be drawn with personal lending, where the bank must ensure that the customer has the ability to borrow.

Means

Means or capacity refers to the borrower having technical, managerial and financial abilities in order to operate profitably and succeed in business.

A corporate borrower should give the appearance of coping with changes in its business and technology, and should have premises, equipment, transport and staff adequate for the planned use of the loan funds.

Its management should be suitably trained and have sufficient experience. Directors and managers should provide a well-balanced team with a suitable spread of skills and expertise, preferably including financial expertise. A one-man business, or a business dominated by a single individual, e.g. an individual who is both chief executive and chairman, should be considered a high credit risk.

Financially, a bank should be satisfied that the customer's business has good financial systems and controls. If there is a history of financial difficulties, the management's record in sorting them out could be significant. Past achievements can give an insight into what could happen in the future.

Purpose

The purpose of granting credit must be clear and acceptable to the lender. A bank should not lend money unless it knows what it is going to be used for, nor for a purpose that it regards as too risky or that it is outside its normal course of business.

Finance for Working Capital

When the intended purpose of an advance is to finance an increase in stockholding or debtors, the bank should consider the liquidity of the borrower's business. A risk in lending to finance working capital is the possibility that the borrower could require increasing amounts of financial assistance over time, even when it is trading profitably. This could occur when the customer's business is growing at a fast rate.

Growth in business will result in more stocks and more debtors, even when normal trade credit terms are applied. These must be financed, and a bank could be willing to provide some of this. However, credit should not be given to support excessive business growth. For example, when an airline with a fleet of 20 airplanes asks for credit to buy one extra plane to expand its services, its reasoning might appear sound. However, a request from the same company for credit to buy three extra planes should create doubts in the mind of the lender or supplier because the anticipated growth could be too rapid and difficult to manage successfully.

Finance for New Business Ventures

All new ventures are risky, and although many succeed, a considerable number fail. Loans for this purpose are always high-risk, and generally should be referred to a specialist lender, such as a venture capitalist.

Finance to Repay Existing Debts

A bank could decide that, with good security and a high rate of interest, it would make a loan to enable a customer to pay off existing debts, e.g. to pay taxes, dividends or trade debts. However, loans for this purpose are unusual and a bank should question the customer's reasons for needing to settle its other debts. The bank would in effect be giving money to pay off its customer's other creditors, and would itself become the company's main creditor.

Amount of the Loan

The amount of a loan should be consistent with the purpose for which the money is required. It should not exceed the capacity of the customer to repay in full and on time. The amount borrowed should not be excessive, given the size of the customer's business and the customer's equity stake.

The lending proposition must state exactly how much the customer wants to borrow. It is not for a bank to suggest how much it would be willing to lend the customer. However, the bank will check that the customer isn't asking for more than is needed. This is especially important when an overdraft is requested.

The bank also must check that the customer has not asked for too little; otherwise the bank will be in the position later of having to lend more simply to safeguard the original advance.

Example
Center Bank agrees to advance $100,000 to Alpha Inc., a business customer, only to find that Alpha comes back several months later asking for a further $75,000 because it underestimated its borrowing requirement. Center Bank is then faced with the choice between lending the extra money to keep Alpha's business afloat, or taking action against Alpha to recover the money it has advanced already. The bank would prefer to have considered Alpha's proposition as a request for an advance of $175,000, and to have made its original lending decision accordingly.

The most suitable methods for determining whether a customer has asked for a sufficient amount are

- by studying budgets and cash flow forecasts that have been prepared by the customer
- analyzing the balance sheet of the customer, to assess its probable working capital position after the advance has been made, to judge whether more finance might be needed than the customer has asked for
- examining the business plan for the customer's proposed project.

If the bank suspects that the customer will still be short of cash after the loan has been made it should suggest that the lending proposal should be revised and re-submitted for a more realistic amount.

When considering the amount of the advance, the bank also should assess the equity contribution that the customer might have to put towards the transaction itself. There are several reasons why this makes good sense.

A bank should not be expected to provide risk capital when it lends. If an investment by the customer goes wrong, and the customer has none of its own money in the investment, the loss would be borne by the bank in its entirety if the customer cannot repay the loan. By contrast, if the customer has a substantial financial stake in the investment, losses will be borne by the customer before the bank's stake is endangered.

As a general guideline, a bank should not lend more money to a business customer than the customer has invested, even when the bank has obtained adequate security.

Repayment

The source of repayment must be known before any loan is granted. The ability to repay is vital and evidence of this ability ideally should be demonstrated by the borrower's cash flows in the past, or by cash flow projections for the future. In the case of corporate lending, the primary source of repayment for a loan is normally the activities that the loan will finance, typically the cash flows from normal trading operations or from a specific project.

In order to check the likelihood of the customer being able to repay the advance, the banker must do three things

- calculate what the repayments with interest will be. In the case of a term loan, this means estimating the amount of the regular repayments of capital with interest. In the case of overdrafts, this means checking that the customer will have enough cash income in the future to pay the interest costs and will be able to reduce the size of the overdraft gradually.
- obtain evidence that the source of repayment will be sufficient, e.g. proceeds from an asset sale or operational cash flows. The repayment source must be clear from the outset. An assessment of the customer's ability to repay is fundamental to the lending decision. This assessment is the basis of credit analysis, one of the key activities in credit management.

- check the budgets and management accounts of the customer, to supplement the evidence obtained from the bank's own credit analysis of the customer.

At this stage it is useful to focus on repayment a little more.

"Interest and principal are repaid from cash. An elegant balance sheet does not repay the loan, but cash does." E. Altman in *Handbook for Banking Strategy*, ed. Aspinwall and Eisenbeis.

A corporate borrower usually should be expected to pay interest and repay loan principal out of the net cash income from trading operations (operational cash flows). Cash flow analysis is described more fully in *Corporate Credit Analysis*, another title in this series, but a brief introduction will be given here.

Operational cash flows consist of cash receipts from selling goods or services to customers, and cash payments for the purchase of goods and services from suppliers, and for wages and salaries, including income tax payments. Cash receipts normally should exceed cash payments, to give the company a positive net inflow of cash from operations. Operational cash flow is not the same as trading profit, but in the long term at least, profitable companies should have a net operating cash surplus. Loss-making companies could have either an operational cash surplus or negative net cash flows.

Operational cash flows are used to make other essential payments (priority payments) that, if not made, would result in the liquidation of the company.

These priority payments include interest on loans and the payment of corporate taxes. If a company does not have enough operational net cash inflows to pay for these priority items, it must borrow to cover the deficit if it is to avoid collapse.

A company also must continue to invest in new or replacement equipment. Capital investments are discretionary items of spending, in the sense that they often can be postponed. In the long term, however, some capital expenditure is essential. A company with a healthy financial position should have sufficient surplus cash from its trading operations, after making its priority payments, to pay for much of its capital expenditure program.

A bank should focus its attention on how strong a company's cash flows appear to be.

	Item	Comment
	Net operational cash flow	Should be positive
-	Priority payments	
=	Cash for discretionary spending	Normally should be positive
-	Investment spending	
=	Cash after investment spending	If negative, the company must obtain money from non-trading sources, perhaps by borrowing

Good Times and Bad Times

Many companies go through periods of growth followed by periods of decline and cutback, within the general business cycle for their industry. In the early 1990s, many companies experienced a severe downturn in business and had to cut operational expenditures to remain cash-positive. Many bad loans are granted in relatively prosperous times because banks do not consider, or expect, customers' businesses to do other than thrive. Bankers should try to anticipate the effects on their corporate customers of such a decline in business, and question whether their cash flows are strong enough to withstand any foreseeable future downturn. It is important to ask what should happen to a customer's cash flows if sales volumes decline, or if its sales volumes were to increase.

A good times/bad times assessment of cash flows can be attempted. This is a judgment of whether the customer's cash flows will be positive or negative, before and after capital spending, in good times and bad times for trading. There are six categories into which a company could fall, depending on whether net cash flows are positive or negative.

The guide for analysis is shown in the table below.

Cash flows positive or negative

Good times (prosperity)						
Net operational cash flows after payment of priority cash flows	+	+	+	+	+	-
Net cash flows after capital spending	+	+	-	+	-	-
Bad times (decline or recession)						
Net operational cash flows after payment of priority cash flows	+	+	+	-	-	-
Net cash flows after capital spending	+	-	-	-	-	-
Category	1	2	3	4	5	6

\+ *positive net cash flows*

\- *negative net cash flows*

If a company can achieve positive net cash flows after payments for priority items, in both good times and bad times, it should be financially sound and a low credit risk. Capital expenditures, if necessary, always can be deferred.

If a company cannot achieve positive net cash flows, after payments for priority items, in bad times as well as good times, it should be considered a high credit risk.

Companies in categories 1, 2 and 3 in the table therefore should satisfy a banker as to credit risk. Companies in category 1 might never have to borrow. Companies in categories 5 and 6 should be refused credit because they are unlikely to save enough cash during good times for trading to cover their net cash losses in the bad times. The problem category for lending decisions is category 4. A company might achieve positive cash flows in good times, but suffer negative cash flows in bad times. Bankers should expect these companies to build up their financial strength when times are good, for example by accumulating and investing cash. However, if the company needs to borrow, and a bank agrees, the bank must recognize that if the company's business suffers a period of decline, more lending might have to be provided to keep it afloat until an upturn.

Analyzing the potential variability of cash flows in this way can help the banker to focus his or her attention on this key credit risk consideration.

Term of Borrowing (Credit Period)

The length of the loan or credit period must be suitable and appropriate. A long credit period adds to the lender's or supplier's risk. For short-term borrowing, it is usual for a bank to arrange a line of credit. This specifies the maximum amount of credit that the customer can take, in the form of an overdraft or other financing arrangement.

Traditionally, banks have been short-term and medium-term lenders. However, in recent years there has been a move to provide longer-term loans, e.g. commercial mortgages and business development loans.

Banks can make a distinction between

- asset conversion lending
- cash flow lending
- asset protection lending.

Asset conversion loans are short-term, self-liquidating loans to finance a temporary build up of current assets. They are appropriate for companies with a seasonal business, needing to finance a high level of inventory and accounts receivable (debtors) for a short period during the year. A manufacturer specializing in Christmas decorations would be an example.

A bank that makes an asset conversion loan should expect the loan principal to be repaid quickly out of the operational cash flows from the peak seasonal trading.

Cash flow lending is medium-term lending to finance permanent working capital or investment activities. The borrower's operational cash flows should be sufficient to cover interest payments and the repayment of the principal. The borrower's ability to repay therefore depends on the strength of the company's operational cash flows.

Asset protection lending is short-term lending to finance a company's long-term needs for working capital. A difficulty for the borrower could be insufficient profits and cash flows to repay the loan quickly enough, without serious liquidity problems. If the company cannot repay the loan without disruption to its trading operations, a bank might provide an evergreen loan. This is a short-term loan that is continuously rolled over. Repayment of the loan principal would not be expected so long as the company is a going concern. The bank would have to feel confident, however, that the company could repay the loan if necessary from the liquidation of the assets being financed by the loan. Evergreen loans can be secured or unsecured, depending on the financial strength of the borrower and the quality of the assets being financed.

The most common use of asset protection loans is to finance working capital of businesses such as wholesalers, commodity traders, and import and export merchants, where the nature of the business is to make small profit margins as an intermediary, on a high volume of turnover. Such a business needs a large amount of working capital to finance a large volume of stocks.

Asset Conversion Loans

Features relevant to credit analysis	
Purpose of loan	To finance a seasonal build-up of current assets
Source of repayment	The successful conversion of the current assets into cash at the end of the peak sales season
Risks	Failure of the company to have a successful sales season because of poor demand, production delays, distribution difficulties, etc. The company would be left with unsold stock
Protection for the bank	The quality (liquidity) of the assets. The capabilities of the company's management
Loan structure	A line of credit with the customer able to borrow on demand up to the agreed limit Alternatively, short-term loan notes

Cash flow Lending

Features relevant to credit analysis	
Purpose of loan	To provide medium-term finance for the permanent capital of the business
Source of repayment	Cash flows from operations over time
Risks	Inability to generate the anticipated cash flows, because of poor profitability or poor management of working capital by the borrower
Protection for the bank	The company's trading position, stability of profits and financial strength. Loan covenants would give the bank an opportunity to monitor the company's performance regularly over the loan period
Loan structure	Medium-term loan (five to ten years). Banks often will be willing to renew such loans if the company demonstrates its ability to service the debt

Asset Protection Lending

Features relevant to credit analysis	
Purpose of loan	To finance a permanent level of current, and readily marketable, working assets
Source of repayment	The loan may be evergreen where no repayment term is agreed in respect of the capital at the outset of the loan
Risks	The realizable value of assets might fall to less than the amount of the loan
Protection for the bank	The value and marketability of the assets being financed (for both secured and unsecured loans)
Loan structure	Possibly short-term notes

Insurance

In this context, insurance for the borrowing refers to security. Security can be an important consideration in a lending decision. For high-risk loans, or high-value loans, a bank often will want the reassurance of an alternative source of repayment in case the customer's plans go wrong and the loan cannot be paid from the intended source. In other words, a bank must ask what its position would be if the customer failed to make the repayments as planned. Security provides a safety net for the lender in case things do go wrong.

Adequate security should not be the reason for agreeing to lend. It should be regarded by the lender as credit insurance, but not the most likely source of repayment.

Historically, bankers relied extensively on security when lending or undertaking risk. Security is a form of insurance policy that can be called on if the credit assessment were wrong and the customer is unable to meet loan repayment obligations. During the 1980s customers in several countries found unsecured lending was readily available from the banks. But following the recession, they saw a change in the attitude of banks, and unsecured lending was much harder to obtain. The introduction of capital adequacy rules for banks and large amounts of non-performing loans and bad debt write-offs, have resulted in banks adopting more prudent lending policies.

If a bank requires security as a condition of an advance, it must

- establish whether there is any security available, and
- if so, whether it could be sold off fairly easily, should the need arise, for an amount sufficient to cover the loan.

As a general rule, the current value of a security must provide a sufficient margin over the amount of the loan to ensure that if the security subsequently falls in value, the proceeds on realization would still be enough to pay the amount owed.

Property often has been regarded as good security, but banks are now wary given the problems that arose in the late 1980s/early 1990s.

- Property prices can fall as well as rise.
- A reduction in price below market value might be needed for a quick sale.
- The bank would incur costs in selling any property.

- If it takes time to sell off a property, there is an implied interest cost for the lender (the bank), that is earning no income from the asset.

If a bank does take security for an advance, it will ensure that the security has been completed, or at least is certain to be finalized, before the advance is made. (Security is considered in further detail in Chapter 9.)

Interest, Commission and Extras

A bank lends money to make money. It must therefore consider the rate of interest at which it would be prepared to lend, and the commission and fees it charges.

The lending policies of most banks stipulate particular rates for particular types of customer and loan, such as four per cent above base rate or the cost of funds for unsecured overdrafts to small companies. In many cases, however, it will be up to the individual banker to decide the required return from a lending transaction.

A loan for a high-risk venture, such as a new business, would carry a higher rate of interest to compensate the bank for the risk. A secured loan to a credit customer of good standing, in contrast, will be offered at a lower rate. This is necessary to some extent, not just because of the lower credit risk, but because such a customer probably can obtain a loan elsewhere, and therefore has the power to influence the price (interest rate) that the bank will offer.

For a lending bank, the risks of non-payment, even with secured loans, have to be compared with the potential profits from extra lending or higher interest rates. Banks lend at higher rates to customers who are considered more of a risk. A blue-chip multinational company might be able to borrow at 15 to 25 basis points (0.15% to 0.25%) above the London Inter-bank Offered Rate (LIBOR), while a smaller company will have to pay more. Even well established companies with a low credit risk rating might have to pay 1-1½% above the bank's base rate, and higher rates are charged for others.

The ability of banks to lend is restricted by regulations, known as the Basle Agreement or BIS rules that govern their minimum acceptable level of capital adequacy. Because of these regulations, banks are unlikely to lend to high-risk borrowers, and are more likely to ask for even higher interest rates if they do.

Commissions and fees simply refer to any other costs that may be levied as a result of the lending transaction, for example, legal commitment and valuation fees.

Loan Review

Once a bank has granted a loan, it will carry out regular loan reviews. This involves

- a continual analysis of the customer's financial position, e.g. regular credit analysis, and
- tracking the customer's payment record in servicing the loan.

An overdraft facility will be reviewed periodically. If problems arise, the bank could decide to refuse to renew the facility, or reduce its size.

Summary

Every lending bank should use a list of principles when making credit decisions. These principles, that are provided below, are useful in summarizing a banker's approach to credit decisions. They can, in large part, be applied to all credit decisions, not just to lending by banks.

- Banks should seek to lend securely, not to seek growth and a bigger loan portfolio.
- The purpose for which a loan will be used should generate the money to repay the loan.
- Ideally, every business loan should have a second source of repayment in addition to operational cash flow. However, security

is not a substitute for repayment and banks should not place too much reliance on security as a fallback. All companies suffer to some extent from a business cycle of downturn followed by upturn.
- The borrower must seem to have a good character.
- The lending banker must not harbor any self-doubts about the loan; otherwise the loan should be refused.

At the same time, all lending involves some risk, and banks must accept this as an inevitable part of their business. Lending to small companies is usually more risky than lending to large companies. Banks are expected to lend to small companies and are compensated for the risk by charging a higher rate of interest.

Loans will be more risky during a downturn, and the ability of a customer to survive should be considered before a loan is granted. Bankers should try to get to know the business and the senior management of their customers, as part of the process of developing a bank-customer relationship as well as improving credit-risk assessment.

Credit Policy: Credit Vetting

There should be an established credit policy within which credit management operates. A company's credit policy could be contained in a formal document approved by the board of directors; alternatively it could be an informal policy under the control of the chief executive or finance director. Whether policy is expressed formally or informally, there should be rules for how credit is granted and who should be responsible for applying them.

Credit Limits

An important element of credit policy should be to set a limit, decided by top management, about how much credit the company should grant. This limit should be the amount of debtors that the company, given its size and annual sales turnover, can safely afford without risk to its operational cash flows.

Suppose, for example, that a company has annual sales turnover of $1 million. If it has debtors of $100,000, this could seem reasonable and financially safe. Even total debtors of $200,000 or $250,000 might not be excessive. However, if debtors were to be $500,000, representing one half of annual sales turnover, there would be serious doubts about the company's ability to control credit and to collect the money due from its customers.

A policy for the total credit limit could be formulated in several ways.

One approach would be a policy statement that total debtors must not exceed a certain amount, either a fixed money amount of debt, or a percentage of annual sales turnover. Alternatively, a limit could be specified for the maximum amount of days' sales outstanding (DSO) that is described in Chapter 8.

In the example above of the company with annual turnover of $1 million, credit policy might be expressed as a maximum amount of debtors of $150,000, or 15% of annual sales, or as a maximum average credit period of 55 days.

A company also could formulate a policy for restricting customers who are allowed credit. Limits could be set on the amount of credit that should be granted to a particular category of customers, such as those in the same industry or the same country. Banks, for example, could refuse new loans to customers in a particular industry or could give a policy directive that certain types of transaction or certain types of customer ought to be preferred above others.

Other Credit Policy Issues

A company should determine, as a matter of policy, its normal credit terms to customers. For example, company policy might be to ask for payment within 30 days of the invoice date, i.e. 30 days net. All customers should be offered these terms, with exceptional cases referred to senior management.

Responsibilities for credit decisions, credit vetting and monitoring, debt collection and customer liaison should be assigned to specific individuals. Joint responsibilities must not be permitted; otherwise credit decisions by one individual could be overturned by another.

Credit policy therefore should define

- limits to how much credit each such person can give, i.e. levels of authority
- settlement terms, i.e. normal credit terms
- which individuals have authority to grant credit

- which individuals are responsible for monitoring accounts and liaising with credit customers
- which individuals are responsible for collecting payments, and
- overall responsibilities for the implementation of credit policy.

Credit policy should be realistic and manageable. Without realistic credit limits and settlement terms, for example, there will be operational pressures to break policy rules. A manageable policy depends on cooperation between credit control managers and sales and marketing staff. Credit controllers are more likely to be risk averse, while sales staff are more likely to favor granting credit to win sales. A constructive balance between the desire for profits and the need to contain the credit risk therefore is essential.

Credit Vetting

Credit vetting is the process of assessing customer applications for credit. There should be a systematic approach for deciding individual credit limits that treats all customers fairly. A variety of assessment methods can be used that seek to obtain or analyze information about the financial strength and creditworthiness of the customer.

When a bank lends money, or a supplier gives credit to a customer, credit analysis is used to judge the risk involved and the likelihood that the borrower or customer will pay what is owed on schedule. The purpose of the analysis is the same in each case, to judge the liquidity of the company. This involves a study of the business, its markets and market position, its management, and its financial situation.

A company may carry out credit analysis of a potential supplier of a scarce or a particularly important item in order to ensure that the supplier will survive to meet its contractual obligations. Some major companies carry out a credit analysis of banks they might use to borrow money or to deposit cash.

Corporate Credit Analysis

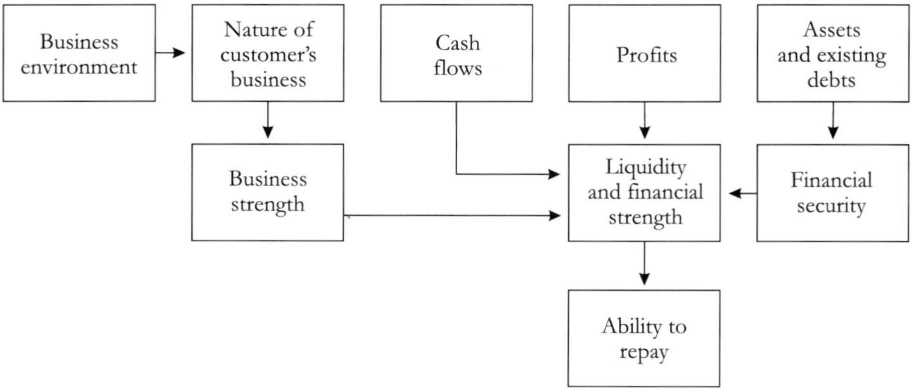

Credit analysis is just one part of the credit control process. Within a trading company its main purpose is to provide information for deciding

- whether to accept an order, and
- if so, how much credit (time and amount) to allow, and
- over time, whether credit terms and limits to each customer ought to be altered.

Credit Analysis of Customers

Banks, suppliers and specialist credit-rating organizations analyze the financial performance of a company by means of financial ratio analysis. However, a wide range of different financial ratios is selected and used by each organization.

Whatever ratios are used, analysts will look at four areas of performance.

- *Liquidity.* Will the company have enough cash in hand to meet its short-term debt obligations when they fall due?
- *Profitability.* Is the company making sufficient profits? Operating profits should be its main source of cash to meet its repayment obligations.
- *Financial gearing.* To what extent is the company financed by equity and its creditors? Is the company over-borrowed?
- *Activity.* Is the company utilizing its working assets efficiently, or

does there appear to be an excessive investment in stocks and debtors relative to the volume of sales turnover?

A financial ratio analysis of a customer could be restricted to an analysis of its annual accounts, using information that is already several months out of date when published. A bank could insist that some customers provide current financial information from their internal management accounting or financial accounts systems, to give the bank more up-to-date information in order to monitor their financial position.

Financial ratio analysis is used extensively for credit analysis, but it has important limitations.

- Simple ratio analysis does not provide much guidance of credit risk. Each ratio is interpreted separately, and there is no proven system that can combine several ratios mathematically to produce a reliable credit rating score for the customer.
- The interpretation of ratios is subjective, and depends on the lender's judgment.
- The indications from one ratio might be contradicted by those from another ratio.
- Credit analysts might not have any guidance as to the relative importance of each ratio.
- For lend/don't lend decisions, ratio analysis does not usually produce a clear yes or no answer for the lender.

Credit Scoring

Companies and banks might assess credit requests from individuals and small businesses by using a system of credit scoring. Credit scoring is the use of statistical techniques to measure the likelihood that a loan application will be a good credit risk. "It is based on the fact that it is possible, using statistical techniques, to predict the future performance of groups with particular characteristics from the past performance of other groups with the same characteristics; and is one of the most consistent, accurate and fair forms of credit assessment available." *Guide to Credit Scoring, 1993.*

More sophisticated tests have been created for corporations, including

"Z" scores (failure prediction scores) and ratings awarded by specialist agencies such as Moody's, Standard and Poor's and Fitch IBCA.

The methods of credit assessment are explained in the two other titles in this series, *Measuring Credit Risk* and *Corporate Credit Analysis*, and therefore are only briefly explained here.

Credit Analysis of Suppliers

A commonly held view of the customer/supplier relationship is that the customer should negotiate a low price and defer payment for so long as possible, in order to optimize profits and cash flows. However, efficient cash management and tough negotiations on price by the buyer, all at the expense of the supplier, should not be allowed to drive the supplier into liquidation.

In some companies and industries, the nature of the buyer-supplier relationship has changed with the adoption of just-in-time (JIT) production and purchasing. The JIT concept, (previously discussed in Chapter 2), calls for minimizing inventory by prompt delivery of materials to the specified quality standard. This involves selecting a long-term single preferred supplier for each major purchased component or raw material item, and abandoning competitive tendering between several suppliers to obtain the lowest possible price. Quality and reliability are more important.

Establishing a long-term relationship with a supplier is an essential part of adopting JIT methods and requires a financially strong supplier. Credit analysis can be used to monitor the financial position of a supplier. In this way a company can determine whether the supplier is likely to continue in business, without appearing to make excessive profits at the expense of customers. Taken to its extreme, this portrays the supplier-customer relationship as a partnership rather than an arms-length business relationship.

Credit vetting occurs at the beginning of the credit cycle. Management of the credit cycle, from acceptance of a customer's order on agreed credit terms up to payment by the customer, is the subject of the next chapter.

Managing the Credit Cycle

The credit cycle is the sequence of events from the time a customer places an order to the time that payment is received. (The cycle begins again when the customer places another order.) The stages in the cycle are illustrated below.

The overall credit cycle has two component parts

- an order cycle that is the sequence of events from the placing of an order by a customer to the delivery of the goods or service and the issue of the invoice
- a collection cycle that describes the sequence of actions from issuing the invoice to receiving payment from the customer.

The credit cycle and its component parts, the order cycle and collection cycle, can be measured by time.

Why Speed up the Credit Cycle?

The credit cycle should be controlled. If it is too long, measures should be taken to speed up the process. There can be several benefits from speeding up the credit cycle. Most important is the need to keep cash coming into the business, to maintain liquidity and have sufficient money to pay current expenditures. During the credit cycle, money is spent producing goods or services for the customer, i.e. a business has to incur cash expenditures to make a sale and create a debtor. If customers

Stages in the Credit Cycle

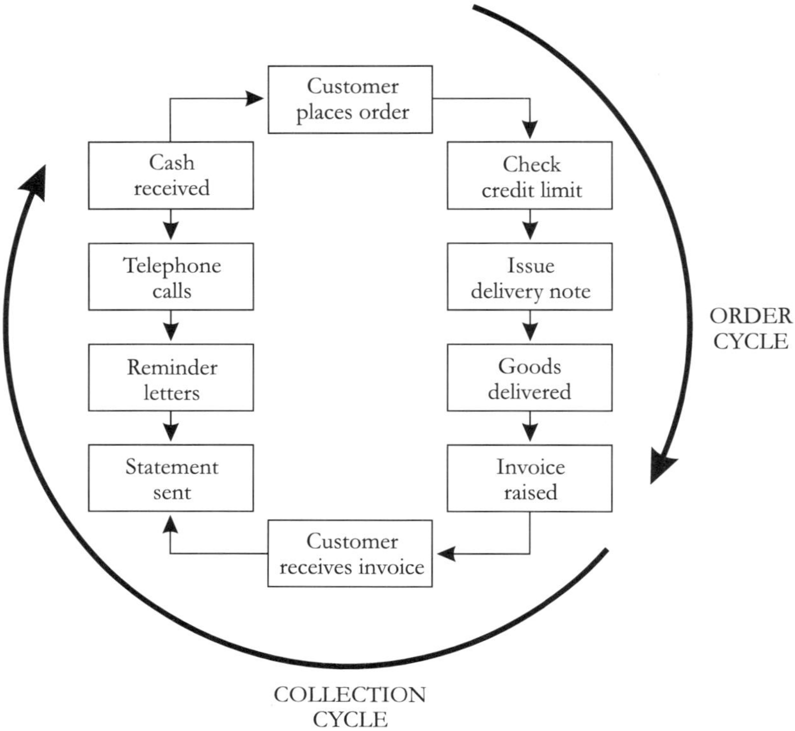

are given time to pay, there is also an interest cost for the money spent that increases with the length of the credit period. A credit sale therefore can be described in cash flow terms as an initial payment to provide goods or services to the customer, a cost of interest during the credit period and an eventual recovery of this cash (with profit) when the customer eventually pays.

A cash flow profile for an individual credit customer is illustrated in the diagram opposite, in which there is a negative cash flow when goods are produced, and an interest cost, increasing over time, until the goods have been sold and the customer has paid. The net cash flow will become positive only when payment is received.

The diagram shows the cash flows for a single credit customer. The greater the number of customers, the greater the total negative cash flow

The Need to Finance Credit Sales

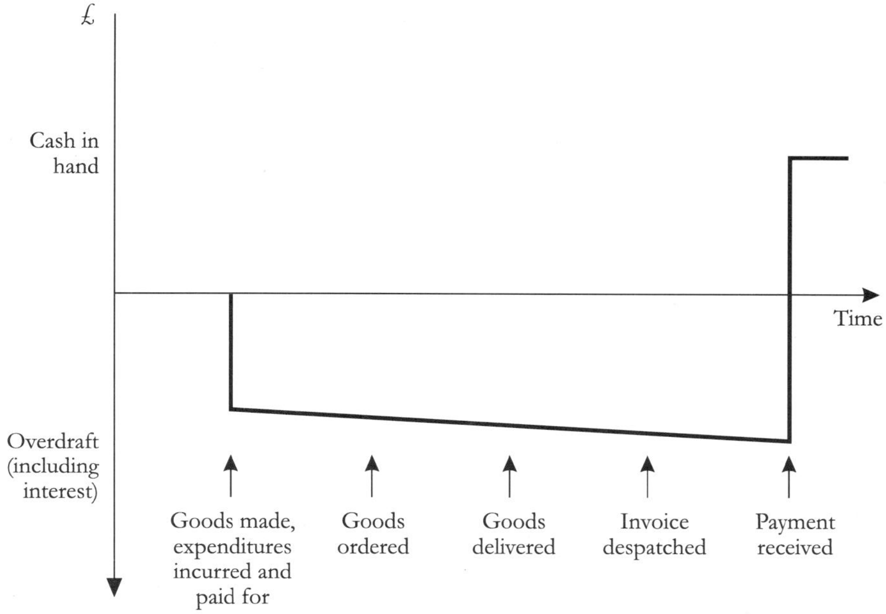

will be. Stocks and debtors have to be financed, possibly by overdraft. This is really a way of stating that a shorter credit cycle will reduce the volume of debtors, speed up the inflows of cash (with profits), improve the company's cash position and reduce the financing cost.

The credit cycle should be neither too long nor too short. The cycle could be too short if customers are not given adequate credit terms. A cycle that is too long, however, could be caused by

- over-generous credit terms
- a slow and inefficient order cycle
- inefficient collection procedures and systems.

Speeding up the credit cycle also can reduce the number of bad debts, because a well-organized debt-collection system reduces the opportunities for the bad payer to get away. Pressure can be exerted on customers to pay promptly and late payments should be chased regularly until payment is obtained.

The Order Cycle

Delays in processing orders and issuing invoices can be outside the direct control of credit management. Goods could be out of stock, for example, a problem about which a credit controller can do nothing.

Credit managers can control some stages in the order cycle. They can ensure that the credit checking process is efficient. Requests for new credit or extra credit should be dealt with quickly. Speed and efficiency in credit vetting can be improved by a continual monitoring and reviewing of customer credit limits.

Invoices should be issued promptly after the goods have been delivered or services provided, and these should be accurate. One of the biggest reasons for collection delays and late payments is the failure to prepare correct invoices. Discounts could be omitted or incorrectly calculated. Invoices can be sent for the attention of the wrong person in the customer's organization. Some companies have begun to issue invoices electronically by electronic data interchange (EDI), a system that can speed up this part of the credit cycle.

Management should monitor the volume and frequency of credit notes. Whenever a credit note is issued to a customer, there is a recognition that the customer, for whatever reason, has been charged too much. The reasons for issuing credit notes should be investigated, with a view to eliminating the causes so that in future queries should be fewer and payment delays shorter.

The Collection Cycle

Efficient procedures and good organization are also needed for cash collection. Collection activity begins with the preparation and issue of an invoice and ends with the receipt of payment from the customer. The aim should be the efficient collection of debts, without risking the loss of customer goodwill in the future.

Typical actions by credit controllers in response to overdue debts are indicated in the diagram below.

Responses to Overdue Payments

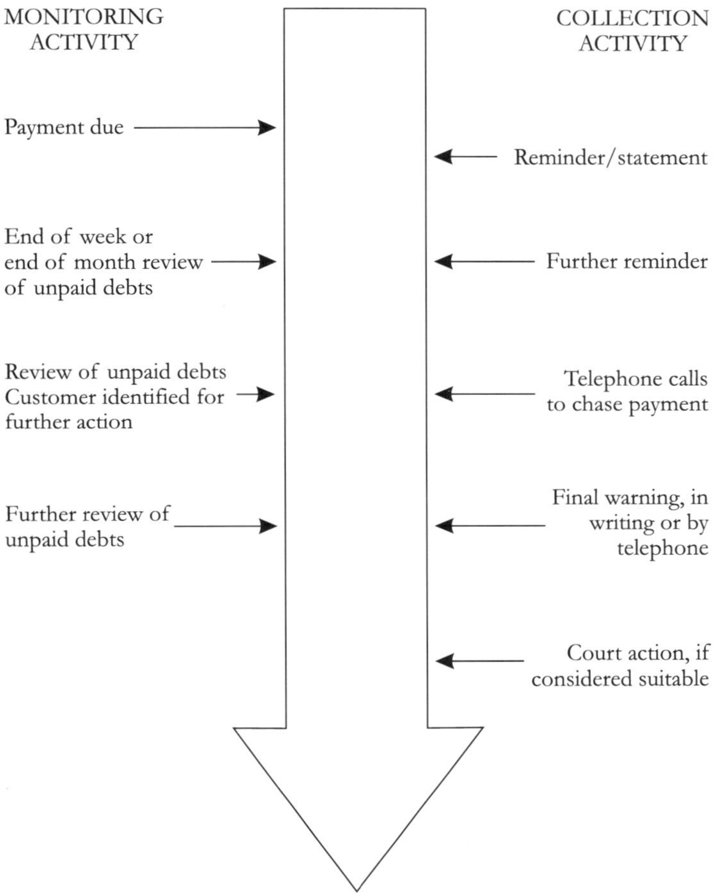

Credit controllers can use computerized diaries that can give prompts to take action on individual customers and to provide reminders for any subsequent action.

Reminder letters can be produced automatically; however, this could cause a problem in that customers who regularly delay their payment could wait for a reminder before bothering to pay. Reminder letters should not give encouragement to late payers, and often they will have to be followed up by telephone calls asking for payment.

For small debts, a company should perhaps question the benefits of reminders and telephone calls. It could be cheaper to write off a small debt and simply refuse any further sales to the customer until payment is received. Management must not, however, allow the volume of small debts written off to become large because the policy of granting credit for small amounts would be called into question.

Credit controllers can be given weekly targets of how much cash they are expected to collect. Debts can be ranked in order of priority and the controller's efforts in collecting payments should focus primarily on the debts with the highest priority. The progress of collecting individual debts should be monitored closely. Problems with late payers and tactics for dealing with them could be discussed at weekly progress meetings under the leadership of the financial controller or finance director.

Some credit controllers take the view that debt collection procedures should not consist solely of action whenever a debt remains unpaid after the due date. A more active approach to debt collection can be adopted through better liaison with the customer. A member of staff in either the finance or the sales department, could be given the task of telephoning the customer soon after the goods or services have been delivered and the invoice dispatched. The purpose of this contact should be to establish as early as possible whether the customer is satisfied with the delivery, that the documentation is in order and that there is nothing to prevent prompt processing and payment of the invoice. Problems then can be dealt with sooner rather than later, and so improve the prospect for prompt payment.

Example

A US company, acting as an agent for a Swedish manufacturer, sold a consignment of weather-monitoring equipment to a customer in Dubai.

The customer was granted credit for a suitable period, but the US company planned that the money from the customer eventually would be used to pay its Swedish supplier, from whom a slightly longer credit term was negotiated.

After the goods were delivered to Dubai, the sales director of the US company learned from the customer that payment could not be made until the goods had been checked. It was not certain how long the checking would take. But because there was no one available to do it, and the consignment of goods had not yet been opened, payment would not occur for some time.

The finance director needed prompt payment from the customer otherwise he would be unable to pay his own supplier. To deal with the situation, he flew directly to Dubai and spent two days opening the consignment himself, checking and counting the goods in the presence of the customer's representative. By telephoning the customer soon after delivery, and being alerted to the problem at an early stage, the US company averted legal action by its Swedish supplier, and the possibility of liquidation.

Query Control

Unless they are properly controlled, customer queries can result in the non-payment or late payment of invoices. The customer could refuse to pay the invoice in dispute, and also other unpaid invoices. This can result in large unpaid balances on the accounts of the customers involved.

Companies could have large amounts of delayed payments from customers while dealing with queries. Suppose a company has customer queries amounting on average to 8% of its annual turnover, and that customers do not pay until queries are satisfactorily answered. Annual turnover is $10 million. If the company could reduce outstanding queries to 1% of turnover, it could reduce its debtors by $700,000 ($10 million x (8-1%)). At an interest cost of 10% per annum, this would create savings of $70,000 per annum.

Efficient query control can be an effective way of managing credit by reducing credit exposures and improving profitability.

The causes that give rise to queries should be tackled by

- delivering goods or services as specified by the customer
- providing goods or services to the quality standard that is expected by customers
- delivery on time
- correct invoicing, as to amount and other details.

Queries could be anticipated by checking, perhaps a week after delivery, whether the customer is satisfied, the invoice has been received and its details are correct. Properly managed, this can help to promote a customer-care philosophy and improve the relationship with the customer. If queries do occur, they can be dealt with sooner rather than later, resulting in speedier payment.

The processing of queries can be organized, possibly by the credit department. Incoming queries can be logged when they are received, and referred to the department responsible for resolving them. Query handling reports can be returned to the credit department as soon as the query has been answered. Any action taken should be recorded in a log. Monthly reports can be produced that would

- show the number of queries outstanding
- give an age analysis of queries, showing how long they are taking to resolve
- provide an analysis of the causes of customer complaints
- summarize the amount of refunds (credit notes) given.

Management can monitor the query-handling process and take action, where appropriate, to deal with the causes of such complaints or the ways in which they are handled.

Liaison Between Credit Managers, Sales Staff and Customers

The sales force should be involved in the credit decision from an early stage. Sales staff can negotiate on price and delivery terms, and also on credit terms. This can help to make the customer aware that the credit terms are part of the deal.

For important customers, credit controllers should know the people to contact, especially the purchase ledger staff. They should also know

- how payments are authorized within the customer's organization
- check run dates
- the credit history of the customer, and in particular the customer's record for late payments.

Monitoring Customer Credit Limits

Credit management should include a system for the continual monitoring of regular customers. The creditworthiness of customers can be reassessed in the light of current information about their payment record. Alternatively, an updated credit assessment can be obtained, either externally, for example from a credit reference agency, or from an assessment carried out by in-house staff, such as a financial analysis of the customer's most recent annual accounts.

Credit terms to customers can be reviewed, and credit limits lowered whenever deterioration in the customer's financial position is suspected. When a customer's credit rating improves, requests for more credit by the customer can be answered quickly and positively, helping to maintain a good business relationship.

In-house Credit Ratings

Credit monitoring can be simplified by a system of credit ratings. For example, a company could have five credit risk categories for its customers. These credit categories or ratings could be used to decide either individual credit limits for customers within that category or the frequency of the credit review.

Guidelines could be provided to help credit controllers decide into which category a customer belongs. An example of a rating system is illustrated in the table on the next page.

Illustrative Customer Credit Ratings

	Rating	Payment record	Financial indicators	Frequency of credit reviews	Credit limit, (as % of customer's annual purchases)
A	Very High Risk	Accounts overdue by 60+ days	Low profits Poor liquidity Highly indebted		Cash only (payment with order)
B	High Risk	Accounts overdue by 30-60 days	Deteriorating profitability, liquidity, or gearing High credit taken ratio	Monthly	Reduce to 10% of annual purchases
C	Average Risk	Accounts overdue up to 30 days	Stable position	Quarterly	15% of annual purchases
D	Below Average Risk	Accounts paid on time	Stable or improving position	Six-monthly	25% of annual purchases
E	Low Risk	Accounts paid early	Strong financial position	Annually	For negotiation with the customer

Payment Records

Over time, the payment habits of a customer can be assessed, and the customer's credit rating and credit limits can be set accordingly. Any deterioration in a customer's payment record could raise concerns about the customer's creditworthiness.

Example

A company categorizes its credit customers into four groups.

Category
1. Prompt payers
2. Those who pay within 30 days of the due date
3. Those who pay between 30 and 60 days of the due date
4. Those who pay over 60 days late

The recent payments record of a regular customer, Victor, is as follows

Invoice number	Date of invoice	Date payable	Payment received	Days overdue
3257	March 7	April 7	April 28	21
3816	June 26	July 26	Sept 1	37
3942	July 19	August 19	Sept 1	13
4185	Sept 3	Oct 3	Nov 5	33
				104

Average days overdue = 26 days (104 ÷ 4).

Analysis
The company would rate Victor in credit category 2. A review of the payment record suggests that Victor delays payment until around the end of the month following the due date for payment. This is quite typical business practice, and although Victor is not a good payer, there is a discernible payment pattern that could persuade the company to treat Victor as an average credit risk.

Credit Taken Ratio

A credit taken ratio can be used to monitor the credit limits of customers. This compares the amount currently owed by a customer with the annual sales turnover in his account.

Example
A company has two debtors, Able and Baker. Each customer owes \$20,000. Annual sales to Able are about \$200,000, and annual sales to Baker are about \$100,000.

Analysis
The credit taken ratio is 10% for Able (20,000 ÷ 200,000 x 100%) and 20% for Baker. Baker could be regarded as a higher credit risk. The company might wish to keep the credit taken ratio for customers below a certain limit. If this limit were 20%, any request from Baker for further credit would be refused until the outstanding debts were settled. However, the company would be willing to consider any request from Able for more credit.

Debt Recovery Through the Courts

Procedures for pursuing non-payers through the courts, or procedures for claiming a creditor's rights in the event of a customer's insolvency are beyond the scope of this book. Briefly, legal procedures must begin with a decision to sue a non-paying customer, and to choose from the legal options available. Credit controllers should be properly trained in legal procedures, so as to be able to deal with claims through the court for small debts. For large unpaid debts, a decision could be taken to put the matter into the hands of an attorney.

Companies with a large amount of bad debts that do not wish to devote administrative effort to legal procedures and court action could use the services of a debt collection agency. It is important to recognize that although it can be vexing to allow a customer to get away without paying, any course of action to collect a debt should not cost more than the value of the debt. It is better to tighten up credit vetting procedures, learn from past mistakes, and try to minimize bad debt levels in the future.

Bad Debts

At some stage, a company must reach a decision about bad debts. A debt can be written off as uncollectable when it is decided that no further action in pursuit of payment would be worthwhile. A bad debt also can become unavoidable when a customer's business goes into liquidation. Occasionally, a decision could be taken to force a non-paying customer into liquidation, although trade suppliers generally leave the decision about liquidation to a bank, the tax authorities or the customer's own board of directors.

Summary

Efficient management of the order cycle and cash collection cycle is fundamental to credit management. Decisions to grant credit presuppose that measures will be in place to collect due payments. Without these, control over the finance cost of debtors and bad debts cannot be exercised effectively.

Organization and Control of Credit Activities

Management should ensure that responsibilities for credit management are allocated, efficient operating systems are in place, and credit control staff are of a suitable quality and properly trained and motivated.

The allocation of credit management responsibilities should recognize the importance of the customer. Credit decisions can affect the company's relationship with its customers. Therefore it is important to establish a close liaison between the credit control staff and the sales force and, throughout the credit period, between the credit controller and the customer.

Responsibilities

Although large groups of companies often will have a centralized treasury department, credit control activities usually are decentralized throughout the group. Within head office, a group credit manager might have responsibility for monitoring the performance of individual local credit controllers throughout the group.

The head office responsibility might be

- to decide overall credit policy, for example, total credit limits for the group, and each company within the group
- to approve and train local credit controllers within the group

- to ensure that local credit control operations are efficient, e.g. using suitable computer systems, and properly staffed
- to monitor local credit control performance through a regular reporting system
- to make major credit decisions, referred up to head office by local management
- to monitor group credit risks where the same customer takes credit from several subsidiaries within the group.

Credit Control Performance Reports

Like any other business function, the performance of the credit control function should be monitored regularly. Management reports can compare current performance with a budget or target, or with a trend over time.

Two key measures of performance are

- days' sales outstanding (DSO), and
- bad debt levels.

Days' Sales Outstanding (DSO)

DSO is jargon for the average number of days a company is taking to collect its debts. It is sometimes referred to as debtor days or the average credit period. A company could set a target DSO for its customers, or perhaps a different target DSO for customers from each industrial sector, because payment patterns can vary between industries.

There are several ways of calculating the average days' sales outstanding. Each method of calculation produces an estimated average credit period, and there will be some differences in the figures produced by each method. Credit analysts normally estimate DSO for other companies from their annual accounts, and base the estimate on the annual sales turnover as follows:

$$\text{DSO} = \frac{\text{Debtors}}{\text{Annual sales}} \times 365 \text{ days}$$

Credit managers usually will calculate DSO for their own company by a different method, more regularly than once each year. Three such methods are

- the 2M method (based on sales for the previous two months)
- the 3M method (based on sales for the previous three months)
- the exhaust method.

2M Method

The 2M method is based on the principle that normal credit terms are 60 days, i.e. two months. The DSO is calculated by comparing the amount of debtors at a given date with sales in the previous two months, as follows

$$\text{DSO} = \frac{\text{Debtors at end of Month 2}}{\text{Sales in Months 1 and 2}} \times 60 \text{ days}$$

3M Method

The 3M method is based on the principle that normal credit terms are 90 days, i.e. three months. The DSO is calculated by comparing the amount of debtors at a given date with sales in the previous three months, as follows

$$\text{DSO} = \frac{\text{Debtors at end of Month 3}}{\text{Sales in Months 1, 2 and 3}} \times 90 \text{ days}$$

Exhaust Method

This method takes the amount of debtors at a given date, and makes the assumption that these relate to the most recent sales. For example, if at the end of June, a company has debtors of $500,000, and its monthly sales are $200,000, the debtors can be matched with sales in the previous months until the full $500,000 is fully allocated (exhausted) and a figure for DSO can be obtained.

Month	Amount of sales	Days' sales outstanding
	$	
June	200,000	30
May	200,000	31
April	(balance) 100,000	* 15
	500,000	76

$$* \quad \frac{\text{Balance}}{\text{Sales in month}} \times \text{days in month, i.e.} \quad \frac{\$100,000}{\$200,000} \times 30 \text{ days}$$

Example

Gamma is a manufacturer of windows. The credit manager has been set a target credit period of 55 days that is considered typical for this section of the building materials industry.

At March 31, Gamma had debtors of $1.8 million. Sales were $450,000 in January, $600,000 in February and $900,000 in March.

Analysis

When setting a target DSO, the company should specify the method of estimation.

Using the 2M method (sales in February and March):

$$\text{DSO} \quad \frac{\$1,800,000}{\$(600,000 + 900,000)} \times 60 \text{ days} = 72 \text{ days}$$

Using the 3M method:

$$\text{DSO} \quad \frac{\$1,800,000}{\$(600,000 + 900,000 + 450,000)} \times 90 \text{ days} = 83 \text{ days}$$

Month	Amount	DSO
	$	
March	900,000	31
February	600,000	28
January	Balance 300,000	* 21
	1,800,000	80

$$* \quad \frac{\$300,000}{\$450,000} \times 31 \text{ days}$$

The three methods provide different estimates. However, all three estimates show that Gamma is failing to achieve its target. This could be because of ineffective credit management; alternatively, the problem could result from deterioration in trading conditions in the building materials industry.

Using DSO Estimates for Credit Control

A DSO target can be set and used, for example, to calculate the amount of payments that must be collected from debtors, for example over the next month, to bring the credit period to an acceptable length.

Example
Returning to the example of Gamma, suppose that the company wishes to reduce the DSO to 70 days by the end of April. Estimated sales in April are $1.2 million.

Analysis
Gamma's credit managers would have a target amount of debts to collect in April if the DSO is to be reduced to 70 days. The amount that must be collected depends on the method used to estimate the DSO.

Exhaust Method
Using the exhaust method, a 70 days' credit period will relate to sales in April and March (61 days in total) and nine days of sales in February (70 days minus 61 days). Debtors at the end of April therefore can include sales for nine days in February, i.e.

$$\frac{9}{28} \quad \text{x} \quad \$600,000 \quad = \quad \$193,000$$

The remaining debtors from February of $407,000 ($600,000 - $193,000) must be collected in April. The target for collections in April is

	$
January sales	450,000
February sales (19 days)	407,000
	857,000

3M Method

Using the 3M method, and taking the estimated sales of $1.2 million for April together with sales of $900,000 in March and $600,000 in February, the target value of debtors at the end of April (to reduce the DSO to 70 days) can be obtained as follows

$$\frac{\text{Debtors}}{\$(1{,}200{,}000 + 900{,}000 + 600{,}000)} \quad \text{x} \quad 90 \text{ days} = 70 \text{ days}$$

$$\text{Debtors} = \$2{,}700{,}000 \quad \text{x} \quad \frac{70}{90} \quad = \quad \$2{,}100{,}000$$

To achieve debtors of $2,100,000 by the end of April, the target amount for collection in April can be calculated as follows

	$000
Debtors at end of March (900 + 600 + 450)	1,950
Sales in April	1,200
	3,150
Target debtors at end of April	2,100
Therefore, target for collections during April	1,050

At the end of each month, the management report on the performance of the credit control function can compare the target for collections in the month with actual collections. Reasons should be given for significant discrepancies between actual performance and the target.

Aged Debtors' Report

Most companies with computerized systems produce a report of overdue debts (aged debtors). An aged debtors' report lists the customers who owe money, the total amount owed and the period of time for which any amounts are overdue. The list can be used to identify customers who should be chased for prompt collection of debt.

The format of the report can vary widely. Some aged debtors' lists include the credit terms as well as the amounts owed by each customer, and show how long each payment is overdue. Other reports simply list the unpaid amounts for each customer and the length of time since the date of the invoice or invoices.

The report can have a comments column, to record any action taken to obtain an overdue payment.

Summary reports of aged debtors can be used to identify weaknesses in the credit control system. A number of sample reports are shown below. They include

- an aged debtors' listing showing amounts outstanding from individual customers
- an aged debtors' exception report that shows the five most significant unpaid debts for a company, and indicates the actions being taken to deal with them
- a summary aged debtors' report showing the total amounts still unpaid, and the number of days that payments are overdue. This report also includes a summary DSO report and shows a collection index. In this example, the report shows the percentage of sales in the previous six months for which payments are overdue.

Aged Debtors' Report

Foxtrot Limited
Data as at: 31/10/98 Report produced on November 5 1998

Customer	Total	Current	1 mth	2 mths	3 mths	4 mths	Comment
	$	$	$	$	$	$	
Alpha	16,000			16,000			*1
Delta	4,500	4,500					
Beta	7,000	2,500	4,000		500		*2
Omega	12,600	5,600	7,000				
Epsilon	15,250		12,250	3,000			*3
Gamma	6,000		6,000				
Total outstanding	61,350	12,600	29,250	19,000	500		

*1 Customer chased by telephone when payment was 45 days overdue (20 October). Payment promised, but not yet received.

*2 $500 of an invoice totaling $4,500 is in dispute. The remaining $4,000 of the invoice has been paid.

*3 Customer chased by telephone when payment was 45 days overdue (20 October).

Aged Debtors' Exception Report

The five largest overdue accounts, overdue by more than 30 days
Data as at November 17 1998

	Name	Last 12 months' sale	Total due	Amounts overdue 31/60 days	61/90 days	90/120 days	Credit limit	Credit taken ratio
		$	$	$	$	$	$	
1.	Brown	150,000	40,000	6,000	14,000	20,000	40,000	27%
2.	Green	18,000	6,000		6,000		6,000	33%
3.	Blue	32,000	6,000	2,000		4,000	8,000	19%
4.	Red	25,000	10,000			10,000	10,000	40%
5.	Yellow	140,000	25,000	15,000		10,000	35,000	18%

Comments: Why Overdue? Action Taken: Basis for Extending Credit

1. Brown — Customer at credit limit. Credit for $6,000 given over one month ago after discussions with customer. Customer being pressed for payments of $20,000. The credit-taken ratio will be reduced to 20%, and the credit limit to $30,000.

2. Green — Customer at credit limit. Credit rating being reassessed.

3. Blue — Payment of $4,000 expected shortly.

4. Red — Court action being considered. Customer has not purchased goods for five months.

5. Yellow — Customer reported serious financial difficulties one month ago. Probable bad debt.

Summary Aged Debtors' Report

Date: October 31 1998

			Amounts overdue			
Sales month	**Total sales**	**Overdue amounts**	**1-30 days**	**31-60 days**	**61-90 days**	**Over 90 days**
	£	£	£	£	£	£
May	345,000	56,000			8,000	48,000
June	421,000	93,500		61,900	31,600	
July	139,000	73,200	12,200	61,000		
August	102,000	60,000	45,300	14,700		
September	187,000	105,400	105,400			
October	285,000	79,000	79,000			
Total	1,479,000	467,100	241,900	137,600	39,600	48,000

Average days' sales outstanding 38 days.
Overdue payments index (as a percentage of sales in the past six months) = 31.6% (467,100 ÷ 1,479,000).

Monitoring Total Credit Limits

An aged debtors' list and an aged debtors' exception report provide control information to credit managers. Total credit limits, as well as individual credit limits and payment records, also should be monitored continually. Senior management should receive regular reports to show whether there is adherence to their policy for total credit limits.

A credit utilization report can be prepared showing the extent to which customers are using their credit limits.

Credit Utilization Report

Customer	**Limit**	**Utilization**	**Margin**
	$000	$000	$000
Alpha	70	66	4
Gamma	200	130	70
Beta	40	39	1
Delta	90	74	16
	400	309	

Total Utilization 77.3%

A report on credit utilization can be used by operational managers to identify customers who might soon want further credit. It can indicate whether the company's policy on overall credit limits could be acting as a constraint on credit sales. A utilization of 90%, for example, would indicate that many customers are at or near their credit limit, suggesting that the company's credit policy is very tight.

Control Reports for the Whole Credit Cycle

One of the limitations of a performance report based on days' sales outstanding is that it does not measure performance for the credit cycle as a whole, only for the collection cycle. The credit cycle starts with the customer placing an order and ends with payment, whereas the collection cycle does not begin until the invoice has been issued. The credit cycle includes both the order cycle and the collection cycle.

Credit managers should be given targets, and reports on their performance could include a comparison of their target and actual figures achieved for

- average length of the order cycle
- days' sales outstanding
- average length of the credit cycle.

Example

Alpha Inc: Debtors Management Report
Month: July 1998

	Target days	Actual days	Comments
Order processing cycle (from order to invoice)	5	14	Some out-of-stock items. Delays in notifying accounts department to raise invoices, now being resolved.
Days' sales outstanding	45	50	DSO reduced from 54 days in June.
Credit cycle	50	64	

Cash Collection Targets

Weekly cash collection targets can be set for each individual responsible for collecting payments for credit customers. With suitable incentives for the individuals concerned, a detailed personal cash collection budget can be an effective method of maximizing and speeding up collections.

Some companies set cash collection targets on a monthly basis for the company as a whole. However, it can be argued that setting a single group target would be less effective than targets for individual credit controllers, itemizing which particular overdue debts each should be trying to collect.

The 80/20 rule often applies to debtors, i.e. 80% of payments outstanding are usually owed by about 20% of customers. Credit controllers should recognize the importance of trying to ensure prompt payment from this 20%, and direct most of their efforts to this task.

A global target for cash collection can encourage credit controllers to chase the oldest debts first, regardless of their value. In contrast, by setting individual targets for cash collection, a suitable balance can be drawn between old debtors and large-value debtors. Individuals can be assigned the task of collecting payments from specific customers and for specific invoices.

Performance reports can be prepared weekly, and reasons for failing to collect specific debts can be explained. An example is shown below. The list of debtors has been kept short for the sake of clarity.

Weekly Cash Collection

Individual: T Crewe
Week ending August 14 1998

Customer	Payment due	Targeted for collection	Amount received	Comment
		$	$	
Alpha	5/8	7,620.45	7,620.45	
Tango	30/6	12,400.00	5,000.00	Part payment. Credit rating of customer under review.
Gamma	31/7	3,271.55	0.00	Two telephone calls.

Victor	31/7	6,025.00	6,025.00	
Orion	30/6	2,400.00	2,400.00	
Baker	31/7	32,500.00	0.00	Customer has promised payment within seven days. Payment being pursued.
Indigo	14/7	15,625.80	15,625.80	
Nutmeg	30/4	950.00	950.00	Payment over 90 days overdue. Letter sent to customer.
Sierra	10/8	17,000.00	17,000.00	
		97,792.80	54,621.25	

Collection ratio 56%

Comment
The failure to collect the debt of Baker is the main reason for the low collection ratio, i.e. the low total amount received as a proportion of the weekly target.

Bad Debts Performance

Credit managers should be held accountable for bad debts. One method of creating accountability is to set a target for bad debts (as a percentage of sales turnover). Actual bad debt performance can be monitored against the target, perhaps every three months. Reasons for significant differences between target and actual performance can be analyzed. Payment problems with individual customers also can be reviewed.

Monitoring bad debt levels should be combined with monitoring days' sales outstanding. Deferring decisions to write off debts as uncollectable can reduce bad debt levels, but DSO would increase as a consequence.

Summary

All companies should seek to manage the credit cycle efficiently. Efficient management calls for good organization, clear targets, well-established systems and procedures and well-trained staff. Information must be readily available, however, to enable credit controllers to monitor customer accounts, and control reports can help to ensure that credit managers are held accountable for the performance of the system.

Security, Guarantees and Covenants

The legal practices and terms used here are based on international law. Some EU laws may differ and legal requirements in emerging markets are still evolving.

Security for a loan, a loan guarantee or a customer's agreement to accept loan covenants can give a bank some protection against the risk of non-repayment of loans. A bank therefore should establish policy guidelines for deciding when these are required as a condition of lending.

Other companies, unlike banks, usually cannot insist on security, guarantees or covenants, but could use alternative methods for reducing credit risk and obtaining greater security of payment. The methods available to other companies are discussed in Chapters 10 to 12.

General Principles of Security

It is useful to appreciate the value of security to a bank as a means of reducing the credit risk with a loan. A creditor can sue a borrower for an unpaid debt, or can present a petition to the court for the borrower's business to be put into liquidation. A secured creditor has an important additional right, however, that is to realize the security, usually by appointing a receiver to arrange the sale of the secured assets.

Security can take the form of a lien, a pledge, a charge or a mortgage.

Lien

A lien gives the bank the right to retain property of the borrower until a debt is paid. With an ordinary lien, the ownership of the property remains with the borrower, although the lender has possession of the property, e.g. a share certificate. However, a banker's lien gives to the bank the right of sale of the item involved, in the event of non-payment of the debt, after giving reasonable notice to the customer.

Pledge

A pledge is a deposit with the bank of goods, or documents of title to goods, or negotiable instruments, as security for an advance. The bank asks the customer to execute a letter of pledge. Legal ownership remains with the borrower even though the bank has possession.

Charge

A charge over assets of a company gives the bank a prior claim over other creditors to payment of its debt out of those assets. There are two types of charge

- fixed and
- floating.

A *fixed charge* is a charge over a specific asset. By its nature, a fixed charge is best suited to fixed assets that the company is likely to retain for a long period. A fixed charge gives legal title of the asset to the lender. A fixed charge over property is created by a mortgage.

A *floating charge* is a charge on a class of assets of a company (both present and future assets) that change over time in the ordinary course of the company's business. A floating charge applies to current assets such as book debts or stock in trade. A floating charge over the undertaking and assets of a company, the most common type, applies to fixed as well as current assets.

A fixed charge is usually a more satisfactory form of security because it confers immediate rights to the lender over identified assets. The borrower cannot sell a charged asset without the bank's consent. A floating charge can be preferable when the current assets of the borrower are easier to sell off than fixed assets subject to a fixed charge. For example, if a company becomes insolvent, it may be easier to sell its stock in trade than its empty factory premises.

Standard Security Clauses

Banks use standard security clauses in lending agreements. These may sometimes include

- a continuing security clause
- an all-monies clause
- a repayment on demand clause
- an indemnity clause.

A continuing security clause ensures that the security covers whatever the borrower owes to the bank at any time, and not just the original loan.

An all-monies clause ensures that the security covers all debts of the customer to the bank existing at any time and on any account. This includes any interest due, and any expenses incurred by the bank in enforcing its security.

With a repayment-on-demand clause the borrower agrees to repay on demand what he owes. This clause can be important because the bank's power of sale over charged property is exercisable only when the money becomes due. The clause allows the bank to demand payment and then sell the charged assets when payment is not forthcoming.

An indemnity clause permits the bank to recover from the borrower all the costs it incurs in taking, keeping and realizing the security. In legal terms, the borrower undertakes to indemnify the bank for these costs.

Debentures and Guarantees

A borrower could be asked to provide a guarantee from a third party as security for any borrowings. Alternatively, a corporate borrower could give a debenture to the bank. A debenture is a legal document in which a company can create a charge over its assets, giving a lending bank various safeguards and powers.

Debentures are most probably the most difficult types of security to value accurately, and the bank will have difficulty in estimating the net proceeds from selling the secured assets in the event of the borrower's insolvency.

- A realization value of 70% for debtors might be realistic.
- Stock realizations are generally poor, because a customer's stocks often are of little value as security.
- Highly specialized equipment may have little resale value except as scrap.
- Liquidators' fees often are high.

Events of Default/Covenants

Most unsecured loan agreements include restrictive covenants to protect the lender. Covenants fall into two broad categories

- quantitative: these impose specific standards or financial constraints on the borrower that the borrower agrees to adhere to for the duration of the loan. A typical loan agreement might include three or four quantitative covenants, and
- qualitative: these are undertakings of a non-quantified nature by the borrower that are designed to protect the lender against loss.

The breach of any covenant constitutes an event of default, and the bank can demand immediate repayment of a loan if it so chooses.

Quantitative Covenants

The most common examples of quantitative covenants are

- a net-worth test
- restrictions on secured borrowing
- an interest cover test

- a minimum net-worth requirement
- a minimum current ratio requirement.

The Net-Worth Test

The net-worth test, also called the debt test, is a covenant that restricts the total amount of debt that the borrower can incur, expressed as a percentage of the borrower's equity capital.

The borrowing company agrees that its total borrowings, excluding any pre-agreed exceptions, should not exceed a given percentage of the shareholders' funds, i.e. of share capital plus retained earnings plus other equity reserves. This limit is normally set at between 100% and 175% of shareholder funds.

Restrictions on Secured Borrowing

This is an undertaking by the borrowing company to restrict the amount of its secured loans. Normally the restriction will be expressed as a maximum percentage of shareholders' funds, typically in the range of 10% to 100%, depending upon the nature of the borrower's business.

Interest Cover Test

This is an undertaking by the borrower that its income before interest and tax (IBIT) will be at least a specified multiple of the total interest payable by the company in a given period, normally a single financial year. Interest cover is the ratio of IBIT to interest charges, and a covenant can specify that this must be at least 2.5 times. This figure can be as high as 3.0 or even 4.0 times interest if the bank wishes to curb excessive levels of debt. A company in a cyclical business with an erratic profit stream could resist an interest cover test as a loan covenant, because the covenant is likely to be breached as soon as the down-cycle produces a poor trading year.

Minimum Net Worth

A company can be required to maintain the value of its shareholders' funds at a minimum monetary amount. For example, a company could undertake to maintain the value of its shareholders' funds at not less than $200 million. Dropping below $200 million would represent a breach of covenant. Most often the minimum net worth is set slightly lower than the borrower's current net worth, as at the beginning of the loan period. This covenant therefore gives an early warning of losses that would represent a threat to the company's lenders.

Current Ratio Requirement

The current ratio is the value of a company's current assets expressed as a multiple of its current liabilities. A covenant can specify that this must not fall below a certain value. A bank can insist on this covenant particularly for businesses that could have liquidity problems. A bank could look for a minimum ratio of between 1.0 and 1.5, to act as an early warning of an impending liquidity crisis.

Qualitative Covenants

Three common qualitative covenants are

- a negative pledge
- a cross-default clause
- a material adverse-change clause.

The Negative Pledge

This is an undertaking by the borrowing company that it will not create a class of creditor that ranks above the lending bank in the hierarchy of creditors in the event of the company's liquidation.

Cross-Default Clause

Banks often will look for additional comfort from a clause requiring that if a company is in default on any one of its loans or banking transactions above a certain value, this automatically will create a default on every other loan or banking contract. This type of covenant is called a cross-default clause. A cross-default clause is usually quantified to the extent that a minimum size of default, typically either 1% or 2% of shareholders' funds or a monetary threshold such as $1 million to

$10 million, triggers the cross default.

Material Adverse Change Clause
Often banks will seek a clause that makes it an event of default if there is a material adverse change in the company's financial position, or in some circumstances, its commercial position.

Example
Some years ago, an airline company arranged a $35 million borrowing ceiling with its banks as part of a financial rescue package. This ceiling was linked to the net worth of the company's net assets that stood at $41 million. Subsequently the company found that about one year later, its debt ceiling was sharply reduced because of the banks' lending terms.

Aircraft with a net worth of about $5 million were sold, reducing the borrowing ceiling from $35 million to $30 million.

Instead of operating at a profit, the company continued to make losses, reported to be up to $10 million per annum. Because losses reduce the net worth of a company, the company's borrowing ceiling fell still further, perhaps by about $10 million, to around $20 million.

Without the borrowing capacity they had anticipated, management was forced to seek new funds to try to keep the company afloat. Eventually the company agreed to be taken over by a larger airline company.

Summary

Banks should not lend primarily because of the strength of the security or loan guarantee offered. However, security, guarantees and covenants are methods for reducing credit risk that banks must consider in their credit policy and as part of individual lending decisions.

Secure Methods of Payment

When a bank is concerned about the credit risk of a borrower, it can

- refuse to lend
- agree to lend, but at a high rate of interest to compensate for the risk, and perhaps on terms that differ from the customer's original proposition, e.g. for a shorter lending term
- agree to lend, but with some protection in the form of security, a guarantee, or loan covenants.

For companies granting trade credit, the options are different. They can refuse credit, and so risk losing the customer's business by insisting on cash in advance. Alternatively, they can arrange a more secure method of payment.

Payment methods that give some degree of security to the supplier can be grouped into two categories

- methods of payment agreed with the customer that provide some security to the supplier, and
- arrangements with a third-party organization to reduce the risk of non-payment by customers that do not affect the customer directly. These arrangements include credit insurance and debt factoring, forfeiting and some credit insurance techniques.

There is a much greater variety of secure payment methods for export sales where the payment risk is more difficult to control, than for domestic sales.

Payment in Advance

The most secure payment method is payment in full in advance of delivery of the goods or provision of the service. To be certain of payment and to avoid the risk of canceled or dishonored checks, a supplier should wait until the funds have been cleared into its bank account before supplying the goods or service.

Full payment with an order is not common, except for initial trial orders and low-value items. Often buyers are unwilling to pay until they have seen the goods and checked that they are satisfactory. Buyers may also need some credit because they do not have the money to pay immediately. When suppliers in the industry normally offer credit terms, insisting on cash with the order will probably result in lost orders, and customers switching to alternative suppliers who are willing to offer credit. However, in some businesses payment in advance is common practice, even for items of fairly high value.

This is not viable for export sales because it is unreasonable to expect a foreign distributor of high-value goods, such as construction equipment, to stock a complete range of products he may take time to sell, yet demand payment in advance. Exporters doing so will immediately lose out to competition. To overcome this the export credit agencies of major economies support Floor Planning, an insurance technique whereby the buyer receives the goods on long credit but must pay eventually and the exporter receives cash on shipment from his bankers.

When payment in advance is agreed with a foreign buyer for an export sale, the buyer could ask in return for an advance payment guarantee or bond. This is a guarantee given by the supplier's bank that it will refund any advance payments or progress payments from the buyer to the supplier, in the event that the supplier fails to fulfil the terms of the contract e.g. fails to deliver the goods. When a bank gives a guarantee or bond on behalf of an exporter, the bank is exposing itself to a credit risk from the exporter. Its willingness to give further credit to the exporter therefore could be affected.

Cash Deposit with Order

A buyer could be asked to pay a cash deposit in advance, with the balance to be paid later, after delivery. For example, for an order priced at $10,000, the supplier could ask for a 10% deposit, with the remaining $9,000 to be paid after delivery. A cash deposit serves two purposes

- it provides the supplier with finance towards the cost of making and delivering the goods or service
- and it reduces the credit risk by the amount of the deposit.

Retention-of-title Clauses

A supplier of goods can specify, as a condition of sale, that title to the goods, i.e. legal ownership, should remain with the supplier, and should not pass to the buyer until the buyer has paid for the goods in full. In the UK, such a retention of title clause in a sales contract is referred to as a Romalpa clause, after an important legal test case in 1976.

Although a UK case, this judgment is applied worldwide and accepted by the International Chamber of Commerce in Paris.

In this case, Aluminium Industrie Vaassen BV versus Romalpa Aluminium Limited, a Dutch supplier sold a consignment of aluminum foil to Romalpa Aluminium Ltd. The sale contract included a clause stating that title to the goods should remain with the supplier until Romalpa had paid for them.

Romalpa became insolvent and the debt was not paid. The receiver appointed to manage Romalpa's affairs claimed that the aluminum foil belonged to Romalpa, not the supplier. However, the court found that ownership remained with the supplier. The Romalpa case thereby upheld, in UK law, the legality of retention-of-title clauses.

In the 1979 Borden case, a quantity of resin was supplied to a customer with a retention-of-title clause in the sale contract. The buyer failed to pay for the resin, but had already used it as raw material in a manufacturing process by the time the supplier claimed ownership. The court decided that the supplier could not claim title to the resin because by this stage it had lost its identity.

A problem can arise when the buyer fails to pay for the goods, but resells them to someone else. The ability of the supplier to use a Romalpa clause to claim the money that the buyer has earned from reselling goods depends on the actual wording of the clause in the sales contract.

The Value and Limitations of Romalpa Clauses

The potential benefit for a supplier of including a retention-of-title clause in a sales contract can be assessed by asking what would happen if the customer went into liquidation without having paid for goods delivered.

In a typical situation, a bank with a floating charge over a customer's assets would apply to the court for an administrative receiver to be appointed. The receiver would then arrange to sell the secured assets, including the customer's stocks, and use the money to repay the bank as much as possible of what was owed. Unsecured creditors would be unlikely to receive more than a small proportion of what they were owed.

If, however, a supplier had delivered goods with a retention-of-title clause in the sales contract, the receiver would not have a claim on the goods. The supplier would be entitled to the return of the goods. In theory, if the goods already have been resold, the supplier can be entitled to payment equivalent to their sale value, but in practice this might be impossible to obtain. Retention-of-title clauses put suppliers, as unpaid creditors, in a better position for avoiding or minimizing the loss.

There are limitations to retention-of-title clauses

- they cannot be applied to the provision of services, unless goods are supplied as part of the service
- a supplier cannot reclaim goods that have been absorbed in the making of another product, such as bricks that have been used to build a house
- the supplier must be able to identify the goods, and prove the identity of same.

Using Retention-of-title Clauses

A company that decides to use retention-of-title clauses as protection against non-payment by customers must make its intention absolutely clear to its customers.

The clause must be included in the wording of the sales contract, and the customer's attention must be drawn to it.

It is important to ensure that the clause is suitably worded. Companies should seek legal advice when using these clauses for the first time.

If a customer goes into receivership, the company must inform the receiver as soon as possible about the retention-of-title clause. An official should then visit the customer's premises to make an inventory of the goods delivered.

Export Sales

Export sales can present a greater credit risk than domestic sales not least because of distance and time. The credit cycle could be extremely long. A buyer might not pay until after the goods have been delivered, and there could be a long delay between the goods being shipped and their eventual receipt by the customer, e.g. length of time in transit and customs clearance delays.

A supplier also could be unfamiliar with the laws, habits and customs in the buyer's country. This can increase doubts about whether the buyer can be trusted to pay and if the buyer does not pay, the supplier then has the additional problem of trying to recover the debt in a country whose laws are probably unfamiliar.

In certain cases, suppliers could have difficulties with exchange-control regulations that prevent or delay a customer paying invoices in a hard currency.

The high credit risks associated with export sales have led to special methods of extending credit and obtaining payment. One such method that can be used for exporting to certain countries is an irrevocable letter of credit. Between 85% and 90% of all world trade is conducted on open account or via letters of credit. It should be noted that letters of credit are always evolving in their use and application, especially in Asian markets.

Letters of Credit

A letter of credit, or documentary credit, is a method of payment agreed between an exporter and a foreign customer that should give the exporter security of payment. The buyer must, however, obtain agreement from a bank to pay by this method. A confirmed letter of credit, that gives the exporter more security than an unconfirmed letter of credit, requires the agreement of two banks.

Payment by letter of credit can overcome the problems of unfamiliarity with local laws and customs, because banks operate in accordance with the Uniform Customs and Practice for Documentary Credits or UCP, an international code of practice formulated by the International Chamber of Commerce. Note that on first presentation, banks reject approximately 90% of letters of credit. This is dealt with in the appendix.

How Documentary Credits Work

The exporter and buyer agree to a sales contract that provides for payment by letter of credit. The agreement must specify whether the letter of credit should be confirmed. Credit risk is much lower with a confirmed letter of credit, and so in certain circumstances an exporter should insist on confirmation.

The buyer asks a bank, often in the buyer's own country, to issue a letter of credit in the exporter's favor. The bank will assess the creditworthiness of the buyer before responding. If the bank agrees to the buyer's request, it becomes the issuing bank for the letter of credit. The buyer is the applicant for the credit and the exporter is the beneficiary.

By issuing a letter of credit, the issuing bank guarantees payment to the beneficiary, provided that the beneficiary complies with all the specified terms and conditions.

The issuing bank must ask a bank in the beneficiary's country to advise the credit to the beneficiary, i.e. the exporter. This bank is known as the advising bank. An advising bank agrees to handle the credit, i.e. do the administrative work in the exporter's country, but does not make any commitment to guarantee payment to the exporter. The guarantee comes from the issuing bank.

For a letter of credit to be confirmed, the advising bank will be asked by the issuing bank to add its own confirmation to the credit. This means that the advising bank is required to add its conditional guarantee of payment to the guarantee already provided by the issuing bank.

If it agrees to confirm the credit, it is then known as the confirming bank or advising/confirming bank. Thus, a confirmed letter of credit carries the conditional guarantees of two banks, usually one in the exporter's country, the confirming bank, and one in the buyer's country, the issuing bank.

Bank charges for a letter of credit are usually borne by the buyer, the applicant for the credit, although the buyer could persuade the exporter to bear some or all of the costs. The question of who pays which costs will depend on the relative bargaining strength of the two parties.

After the goods have been shipped, the exporter must present certain specified documents to the bank named in the credit, usually the advising bank. The documents to be presented are specified by the letter of credit. They will include a transport document, e.g. bill of lading, copies of the invoice and, where insurance is paid by the exporter, a certificate of insurance or an insurance policy. Frequently other documents also are specified. Because the letter of credit makes presentation of these documents a condition of the bank's guarantee, the term documentary credits has evolved to describe the system. The custom and practice of letters of credit is laid down by the International Chamber of Commerce to which all countries and banks subscribe. The current code is Uniform Customs & Practice 500.

The exporter usually will be required to present a bill of exchange with the other documents. A bill of exchange is an order in writing from one person, the drawer, to another, the drawee, requiring the drawee to pay a specified sum of money either on demand or at a specified future date. When payment is to be at a future date, the drawee signs his acceptance on the bill, and the accepted bill then becomes an unconditional promise to pay. The bill of exchange that is used for payment with a letter of credit could be drawn on the issuing bank or another bank, e.g. the confirming bank, depending on the terms of the letter of credit.

A bank, almost always the advising bank, to which the required documents are presented will check them, to ensure that they are in order, and that they have been presented on time. If there is an error or fault in the documents, or if they have been presented too late, the exporter could lose the guarantee of payment from the issuing bank, and the confirming bank. The exporter would then have to rely for payment on the good faith and creditworthiness of the buyer.

The guarantee of the bank or banks can be relied on if, and only if, the documents are in order. (See appendix.)

When settlement is by bill of exchange, the exporter will be paid according to the terms of the bill, e.g. immediately or on a future specified date, and the issuing or confirming bank. Instead of waiting until the maturity of a term bill for payment, an exporter can arrange to obtain immediate payment by discounting the bill with its bank, i.e. selling the bill to its bank at a discount to face value.

These procedures are summarized in the diagram opposite.

Confirmed Letter of Credit: Procedures

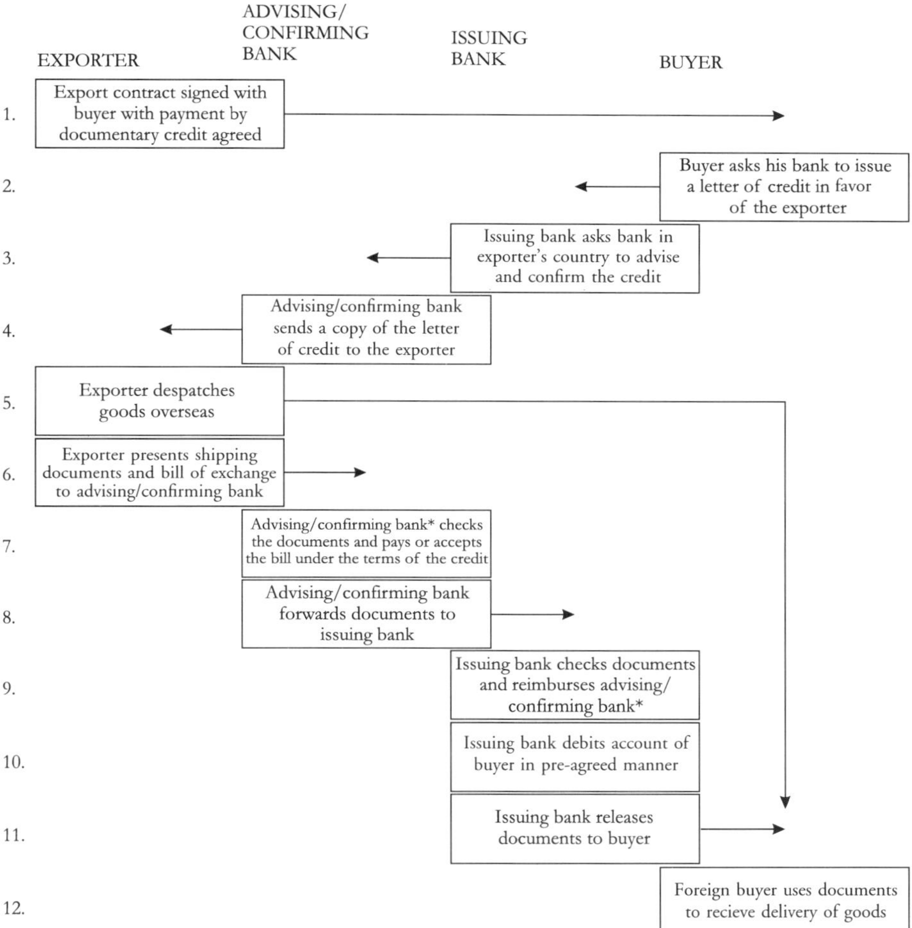

*or another bank specified in the credit

Standby Credits

Standby credits are another form of letter of credit. As their name implies, they are used as a standby, and are called into use only in the event of non-payment by a foreign buyer. For example, they are often used when a foreign importer of goods or services requires protection against non-performance of the domestic exporter. This protection is provided in the form of a standby letter of credit issued by the domestic exporter's bank. In the event of default, the foreign importer can call on the issuing bank for payment.

Example
Alpha Inc. has won a contract to build a pipeline for Beta GmbH, Germany. The German importer requires protection that will guarantee the exporter will perform under the contract, and therefore has requested a standby letter of credit from Alpha's bankers.

Analysis
Alpha's bankers might agree to issue a standby letter of credit in favor of the German importer. This will have an expiry date and be for a maximum amount. In the event that Alpha does not successfully build the pipeline, Beta will make a claim from Alpha's bank by presenting

- a letter stating non-performance
- a bill of exchange drawn on the issuing bank.

If the documents were in order, Beta would then receive payment under the terms of the standby letter of credit.

Forfaiting

Forfaiting is a very flexible form of trade finance that has its origins in Switzerland and Germany. London is now a larger center than Zurich and the technique is very widely used within Europe and for European exporters. It involves the purchase of trade receivables from the holder (beneficiary) on a 100% without-recourse basis. These trade receivables are usually bills of exchange or promissory notes, but can now include book receivables and deferred payments under letters of credit.

Traditionally, forfaiting has been fixed-rate and medium-term (3-5 years), although it can be structured on a floating rate interest bearing basis for periods of up to 12 years and down to 180 days with the minimum amount about $100,000. It depends upon the Aval, or promise to pay, of an acceptable bank in the buyer's country or elsewhere being stamped and signed on the receivable documents. This is a sine qua non.

The trade receivables are, for the great majority of cases, denominated in US dollars, Deutschemarks and Swiss Francs, although other currencies can be considered.

How does it work?

There is no reason why an entire transaction should not be financed but more usually the exporter receives 15% of the sales price as a cash deposit with the balance due in the agreed form of trade receivable. These receivables include an element of interest at a fixed rate that will have been agreed between buyer and exporter for the duration of the repayment period and typically, but not always, will take the form of a series of semi-annual maturities, e.g. five-year repayment term - 10 semi-annual promissory notes.

This series of notes is then sold without recourse to the forfaiter, that is usually a subsidiary of a major bank, who deducts interest at a discount rate. The forfaiter is then responsible for collection and for the debt.

Advantages

To the exporter	To the buyer
• a credit sale becomes cash	• no publicity
• eliminates 100% of risk	• increases borrowing capacity
• rapid processing (simple documentation)	• speeds transaction
• avoids interest and exchange risks	• avoids restriction on borrowing
• frees the balance sheet of liabilities	• cuts administration
• reduces administration	
• finance cost can be factored in up-front	

Forfaiting

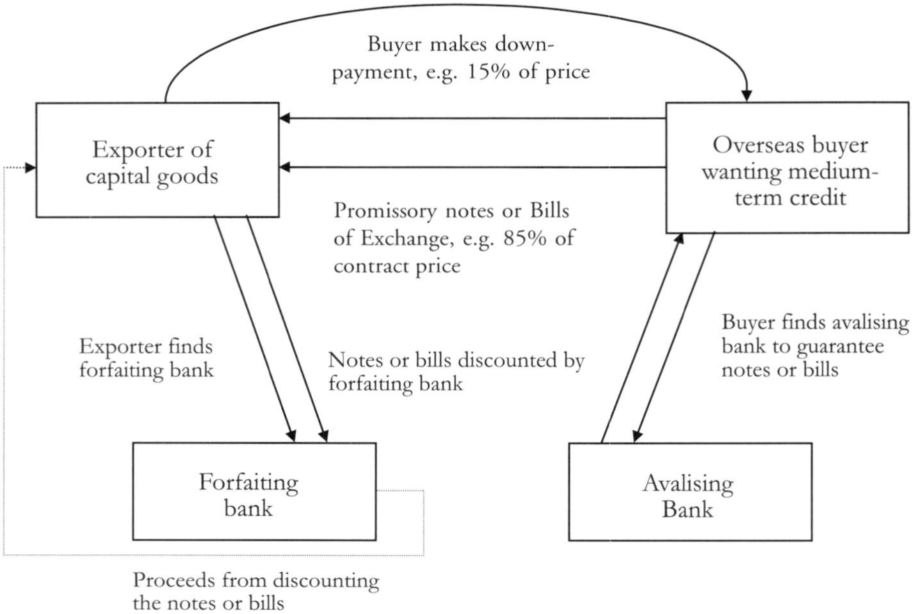

Credit Insurance and Buyer Credits

Historically, credit insurance has not been seen as a completely secure method of payment because, like all insurance, it has to be conditional upon the insured conforming to the terms of the policy. In reality, however, international competition for export business and vastly increased competition between the credit insurers can mean that the payment security is close to that of a letter of credit. Some insurers now take over any debt, having paid the insured, and pursue it. Coface in France is a prime example.

Large exports have long been arranged via a buyer credit, effectively an export-agency-backed bank loan to the buyer. As the exporter ships goods, he may draw on this loan with total security.

Summary

Credit management involves not just decisions about how much credit to grant, but also decisions about what should be done if the credit risk seems too high. Alternative methods of payment could be appropriate.

A cash-in-advance policy can be applied either on a case-by-case basis, for sales to individual high-risk customers, or as company policy for all sales below a certain value.

Companies should also consider the suitability of policies for obtaining protection against non-payment. Retention of title clauses, letters of credit and perhaps forfaiting are examples of methods that can be used. These directly affect the supplier's sale agreement with the customer.

Credit Insurance

Companies insure most of their fixed assets and stocks against events that could result in their loss, such as theft or damage from fire or flooding.

The Purpose of Credit Insurance

Credit insurance protects the holder from non-payment by customers for goods supplied or services rendered. Debts can be insured subject to approval by the insurance company. Credit insurance will help to minimize a company's exposure to credit risk for the debts covered by the insurance policy.

As with all insurance policies, terms of cover are agreed with the insurance company in return for the payment of a premium.

The purpose and the attraction of credit insurance is the removal of credit risk and, often, the provision of bank facilities. This means that

- when an insured debt is unpaid and becomes a bad debt, the insurance company will pay for the loss, but more importantly,
- the profit on a sale becomes predictable and normally free of risk.

Example
Alpha is about to sell goods to Beta on credit at a price of SFr500,000. The cost of the goods is SFr300,000. Alpha is considering credit insurance for the debt, and an insurance company has indicated that it would insure 90% of the debt for SFr150,000.

Analysis

If Alpha chooses to leave the debt uninsured, it should expect to make a profit of SFr200,000 on the sale to Beta. However, if the debt is not paid, Alpha will make a loss of SFr300,000, the cost of the goods. The expected profit will be SFr200,000, but the risk of loss exists.

No Insurance

Expected profit	SFr200,000
Potential loss	SFr300,000

The probability of this occurring is uncertain.

If, on the other hand, Alpha chooses to obtain credit insurance, there should be an insured profit on the sale of SFr185,000, SFr200,000 minus the insurance premium of SFr15,000.

Insurance

If customer pays		**If customer fails to pay**	
	SFr		SFr
Profit on sale	200,000	Cost of sale	-300,000
Premium	-15,000	Premium	-15,000
		Refund from insurance	+450,000
Net profit	185,000	Net profit	135,000

Alpha's choice therefore, is between a probable profit of SFr200,000 but with some possibility of loss, and a certain profit of SFr135,000. The decision whether to insure the debt will depend on Alpha's judgment about whether it is worth paying an extra SFr15,000 to remove the risk.

An insurance company will not insure 100% of a debt, and will expect the client to bear the first part of any loss. This is a normal provision in all insurance policies. The principle remains, however, that credit insurance removes most of the risk so that most of the profit on a sale becomes predictable and risk-free.

What Risks are Covered?

Companies can choose to obtain credit insurance

- for all their sales on a regular basis
- for selected parts of their business
- for occasional, high-value sales.

Credit insurance for domestic sales covers the risk of non-payment by a customer for goods supplied or services rendered, because of the customer's insolvency.

Export credit insurance can provide cover against non-payment under any of the circumstances listed below.

Risks Covered by an Export Credit Insurance Policy

Non-payment in the event of

- insolvency of the buyer
- the buyer's failure to pay within six months of the due date, in cases where the buyer has accepted the goods
- the buyer's failure to accept the goods, provided non-acceptance of the goods has not been caused or excused by the exporter's own actions and the insurance company decides it would serve no useful purpose for the exporter to take legal proceedings against the buyer
- any action by the government of the buyer's country that prevents payment
- war, and similar disturbances that prevent performance of the contract
- in the case of public buyers in the overseas country, i.e. government departments, credit insurance also could cover the risk of failure or refusal of the buyer to perform the contract, through no fault of the exporter
- non-availability of hard currency.

These risks fall into two broad categories, the creditworthiness of the foreign buyer (buyer risks) and economic and political risks in the overseas country (country risks).

There are also risks that are not covered by an export credit insurance policy. These are

- non-payment because of the exporter's failure to comply with the provisions of the insurance policy
- non-payment for causes within the exporter's control
- losses due to a breach of the sale contract by the exporter
- losses covered by a normal commercial insurance policy, e.g. damage to the exported goods, or theft of the goods
- failure on the part of the buyer to obtain the required authority to import the goods or make payment for them
- trading losses on the contract itself.

Under the terms of an insurance policy that covers all the credit sales transactions of a client company, the client will not be required to inform the insurance company about every credit sales transaction. However, the insurance company will impose certain credit limits on what can be insured without its prior approval.

Example

For a first order of up to $2,000 from a new buyer, the company could be allowed to deal freely, with full credit insurance cover, provided that the company has heard no adverse reports about the buyer and has secured a bank reference.

For subsequent orders, the company could be permitted to conduct business with a buyer up to a limit specified in the policy, perhaps around $10,000. However, credit should be granted only on the basis of a satisfactory report on the buyer, obtained from a bank or credit information agency, or on the basis of previous trading experience with the buyer.

Credit limits for higher amounts would require approval of the insurance company. Once a higher credit limit for a buyer is established, it will remain in force for the remainder of the term of the insurance policy.

As stated earlier, an insurance company usually will provide 90%-95% cover against non-payment. The amount of any loss that the insured company must bear varies according to the terms of the insurance contract. For export credit sales, for example, the percentage of the loss that the client company is required to bear could be

- 10% of any loss arising from the insolvency of the buyer, or the buyer's failure to pay within six months of the due date, i.e. losses because of the poor creditworthiness of the buyer
- for non-payment because of economic and political risks in the overseas country, 5% of the loss.

Premiums

The cost of premiums will vary according to the insurance company's perception of the risks being covered.

Example
Gamma has obtained credit insurance from Omega Insurance Company for all its domestic credit sales. Gamma must bear the first 10% of any bad debt loss, and Omega will provide insurance for the remaining 90% of invoice value. The expected level of bad debts from Gamma's credit customers is 1½% of Gamma's turnover.

Analysis
Bad debts are expected to 1½% of sales, and Omega will pay for 90% of the loss. Omega therefore can expect to make payments of around 1.35% of Gamma's turnover (90% of 1½%). A premium of perhaps 2% of turnover might be quoted, giving Omega an expected gross profit margin of 0.65% (2% - 1.35%) of Gamma's turnover.

Credit insurance companies do not take on excessive risks. Because they seek to make a profit on their business, they will refuse to insure debts that, in their opinion, have a high risk of non-payment. Alternatively, a very high premium could be charged to insure a risky debt. The appetite for risk varies with experience.

Advantages of Credit Insurance

Credit insurance minimizes credit risk. As well as providing cover against bad debt losses, an insurance company can assess the creditworthiness of a client's new customers and monitor the creditworthiness of its existing customers, offering advice and assistance to the client. It can advise against giving credit to a particular customer, or suggest when action should be taken on late payment to reduce the possibility of a bad debt.

Credit insurance is not always needed. It should be unnecessary, for example, when a secure method of payment has been arranged, such as a third-party guarantee or, for export sales, a confirmed letter of credit. It is, however, a normal part of commercial practice throughout the US and in much of Europe.

Limitations to Credit Insurance

Some companies have been deterred from credit insurance by its apparent drawbacks. These are

- cost, premiums can appear high, particularly in a recession when bad debts are high
- extent of cover, a credit insurance policy will not give cover for 100% of the value of the debt.

Credit insurance is not always conveniently available at an acceptable price. Changes during the past decade have created a wider and deeper market that is much more user-friendly where an enormous range of risks can be considered. Nevertheless, the average exporter will need specialist guidance.

For export credit insurance, the insurance company normally sets its own limits for country risk, and refuses requests for insurance of exports to countries where it has already reached its limit. However, there is such a wide choice of insurers that this is not a real constraint.

Who are the Insurers?

In the US the leading credit insurance organization is the Export-Import Bank of the US (US Ex-Im Bank) that is given the full faith and credit of the US government. The main programs offered are short-term supplier credit and medium-term buyer credit. Policies cover up to 100% for political and commercial risks.

In the UK, private sector companies dominate the credit insurance business, for goods sold at home and abroad on credit for up to two years. This dominance has existed since 1991 when the government sold its short-term credit insurance business for UK exporters. The state-owned ECGD (Export Credits Guarantee Department) was sold to the credit insurance group NCM. In the UK, leading credit insurers include Trade Indemnity, NCM Credit Insurance, owned by Swiss Re and Coface of France.

In Europe it is a similar story. Private companies such as NCM in the Netherlands, Sace in Italy, Coface in France and Namur in Belgium dominate the short-term credit insurance market.

All major OECD governments provide export credit insurance for capital goods exported on credit terms in excess of two years. Without a state-supported insurance agency, it would be difficult for companies to obtain insurance at an acceptable cost for exports on lengthy credit terms.

Credit Insurance Brokers

Some insurance brokers specialize in arranging credit insurance on behalf of client companies. They take on the administrative burden of finding the insurer who will offer the lowest premium or the best terms of cover, or who will tailor a policy to the specific requirements of the company.

Summary

Insurers provide a credit risk management service. Companies can use insurance to hedge their exposure to credit risk, but for less than 100% of the potential loss.

Insurance reduces the risk of loss, and so makes profits more predictable. However, companies cannot always get the insurance they are looking for on satisfactory terms.

Using credit insurance to manage the risk is therefore a matter for judgment. Companies could choose, for example, to insure exports where sales are on open account terms, but not to insure domestic sales. Alternatively, exporters could ask for insurance against country risks, but not buyer risks.

When insurance is arranged, the credit manager should be satisfied that

- the cover provided is suitable and sufficient
- the premium cost is acceptable
- the benefits of reduced risk justify the cost.

Factoring and Invoice Discounting

A factor is defined as a doer or transactor of business for another, but a factoring organization specializes in trade debts, and manages the administration of a client's sales and debtors on the client's behalf. A company can choose to use a factor to manage, finance and insure its trade debtors.

Services Provided by Factors

There are three services offered by factoring companies

- sales administration, i.e. debtors' administration
- credit protection
- providing finance up to 85% of the value of approved invoices.

These services are available for domestic credit sales, and also for export credit sales (export factoring).

Sales Administration

Companies can use factors to off-load the administration of credit sales. Factors can take on the tasks of recording credit sales in the client's accounting system, e.g. maintaining the sales ledger, sending out invoices, reminders and statements, and collecting payments.

The advantages for the client can be

- cost savings from a reduction in, or elimination of, in-house sales administration
- a more efficient debtors' management system.

Companies can become inefficient in managing their debtors, particularly when they are going through a period of significant business development. For example, business expansion, resulting in a rapid growth in credit sales, could create too much work for a company's existing sales administration system to handle. The company could turn to a factor for assistance, at least in the shorter term, to help it cope with the growth in activity.

Factors also will argue that their efficiency in sales administration should result in a speedier collection of debts. The fee for a factoring service is typically between 0.5 and 2.5% of the value of invoices handled.

Credit Protection

Factors can provide a credit control service for the client company, vetting applicants for credit, and deciding how much credit to allow. When performing this credit control function, factors will also underwrite their client's debts. If a customer of the client becomes a bad debt, the loss is borne by the factor, not the client. This credit protection service is known as non-recourse or without recourse factoring, because the factor does not have recourse to the client in the event of non-payment of a debt by a customer.

For a non-recourse arrangement to apply, the factor must be given full responsibility for credit control. This involves

- approving the amount of credit to individual customers of the client
- continuous monitoring of customers' accounts
- consultation with the client when a debt becomes overdue.

When a debt becomes overdue, the factor will first consult the client. The client could decide to take over the bad debt risk from the factor. If he does, the client must bear any bad debt loss. However, the client has the opportunity to resolve the payment problem without creating illwill from the customer that could otherwise result from the factor's persistent pressure to obtain payment. Alternatively, the client could decide to give the factor the go-ahead to chase the debtor for payment, through the courts if necessary.

A factor is not, however, a debt-collection agency, in the sense that it can be relied on to get money out of customers when no one else can. Factors provide a sales administration service and do not want to get involved with problem customers. Their credit-control system is intended to limit the number of problem customers to a small and manageable amount.

Not every factoring organization will purchase approved debts without recourse and with recourse factoring might be provided, for example, for very large debts. In these arrangements, the client must bear the full loss from any bad debts.

Finance (Advances on Debts)

Companies can arrange to obtain finance from a factor to fund their debtors. Finance can be provided in the form of an advance cash payment for up to 80% of approved invoices. The factor provides cash against the security of unpaid invoices, the client assigns the debtors to the factor.

Example

A factor agrees to advance funds to a client, Baker, against unpaid invoices. The factor will pay 80% of approved invoices. Baker's approved credit sales are $100,000 each month.

Analysis

The factor will pay Baker an advance of $80,000 each month. The rate of interest will be tied to a bank's base rate, but could be a little higher than the client would pay for a bank overdraft.

Baker will receive the balance of the money receivable when the debts are paid, or after an agreed period.

If Baker continues to use the factor's services, there will be a continuous cycle of cash advances, repayments and new advances. Baker, in effect, would be obtaining continuous finance for 80% of its approved debtors. For example, if all Baker's customers pay after two months from the invoice date, Baker would receive continuous finance of $160,000 (2 months x $80,000 per month) that would finance 80% of its balance sheet debtors (80% of $200,000).

The factor also will make an administrative charge, perhaps up to 0.5% of the client's gross annual turnover.

Export Factoring

Factoring services are available for export sales. Export factoring could be used by companies that conduct much of their export trade on open account terms, i.e. normal credit and payment terms, and that do not use more secure methods of payment such as letters of credit.

Export factors work with the assistance of another factor, an import factor, in the country where the debt must be collected.

- The import factor helps the export factor in credit control, i.e. the process of credit assessment and granting credit to the customer
- Payments are collected by the import factor on behalf of the export factor
- Non-paying debtors are pursued through legal action in their own country, with the import factor again providing assistance.

An international network of factors, such as Factors Chain International and the International Factoring Association, allows an export factor to provide a worldwide service for its clients.

Some export factors are willing to provide credit protection, non-recourse factoring, for a client, but usually only if the client asks for it. Protection probably will be provided up to a certain limit only for any individual foreign buyer. Exporters can obtain credit insurance rather than rely on a non-recourse factoring service.

Who Uses Factors?

In the past, mainly smaller companies have used factors; however, some larger companies have also turned to factoring. A factor might refuse to service very small companies, companies in a high-risk market or with a history of bad debts, or companies selling small-value items to the general public, such as mail order firms. The administrative difficulties or credit risks in these cases would be considered too high.

Most factoring companies agree that, for both parties, their service is worthwhile only for those companies with an annual turnover in excess of $250,000 and with average invoice values of $150 or more. In Italy, however, there are more than 80 factors and it is a routine part of business down to very small invoice levels.

Occasionally factoring can be suitable for companies that require specialized sales administration or credit control support for one particular part of their business.

Example 1
A company whose sales are seasonal could find that during the peak season it is unable to handle the credit control function, and can use a factor to assist with the peak load.

Example 2
A multinational company could use a factor to collect debts in one of the countries in which it operates. For example, a US-based multinational company might use a factor for its UK sales administration, but does not use factoring finance.

Example 3
A company could use a factor for credit control or sales administration in a unique segment of the market.

Who are the Factors?

In the US, there are a number of factoring companies, most of which are owned by large banking or financial groups. The top factors are BNY Financial Group, Capital Factors and Century Business Corporation, CIT, NationsBank and Heller Financial. In the UK The Association of British Factors and Discounters provides information about its members. The two leading international associations are the International Factoring Association and Factors Chain International. The latter has more than 300 factoring companies as members in more than 40 countries that cooperate in information and debt recovery.

Advantages and Disadvantages of Factoring

The potential benefits of factoring include

- a more efficient sales administration system
- releasing a company's management from the day-to-day operational problems of sales administration and debt collection
- avoiding the costs of running an in-house sales administration team
- finance to support debtors and thereby support business growth.

Factoring can become more attractive as a source of finance for debtors in the period immediately following the end of a recession. This is because factors offer finance against current invoices, and will be willing to lend more as a client's credit sales business increases. Banks, in contrast, are more inclined to lend against historical criteria, such as the previous year's profits, and are also unlikely to lend more than 35% of the value of a customer's trade debts, against the security of a floating charge.

For an exporter, a particular benefit of using a factor is that it allows the company to deal on open account terms with customers located abroad. This enables the exporter to offer the same terms of trade that the customer expects from domestic suppliers and means the customer does not have to put up with the inconvenience of dealing with bills of exchange or letters of credit.

The potential disadvantages of factoring are

- the cost of the service
- the loss of control over sales administration, in practice the factor will agree procedures in advance.

When a company obtains finance from a factor, the factor takes the debtors as security for the advance. If the company already has a bank overdraft facility, the bank could be relying on the company's debtors as a form of security, perhaps not legal security, in the form of a floating charge over stocks and debtors, but as an element in its decision about how much overdraft to allow the customer. The bank may then wish to reduce the company's overdraft limit. A company should certainly inform its bank when it makes a financing agreement with a factor for advances against debts, in order to maintain a good relationship with the bank.

A company might be concerned that a factor could get too heavy handed when trying to collect debts. One way of dealing with this is to ask the factor for references and to follow these up, before signing up.

Invoice Discounting

Invoice discounting is related to factoring and many factors provide an invoice discounting service. It is the purchase of selected invoices at a discount, and is similar to a factor's financing service. The invoice discounter does not take over the administration of the client's sales ledger, and the arrangement is purely for a cash advance. A client might want to have some invoices discounted only when it has a temporary cash shortage, and invoice discounting would then consist of a one-off deal.

Invoice discounting is confidential. Although a debt is assigned to the discounter or factor, the client's customer is not informed. The customer will become aware of the arrangement only if he defaults and fails to pay the debt.

How Does a Discounting Service Operate?

A company should approach a discounter or factor and ask for a discounting service. The discounter will offer to purchase selected invoices and advance up to 80% of their value.

The client notifies details of its sales to the discounter or factor, often via a computer link, and the discounter or factor then makes an immediate advance against their value.

A facility account is opened with a bank, and all receipts are banked to this account. At the end of each month, the discounter will pay over the balance of the purchase price, less charges, on the invoices that have been settled in the month.

Example

In May, Delta asks an invoice discounter to provide finance against certain invoices. The discounter agrees to finance 75% of their value that totals $400,000. Interest on the advance is to be at 10% per annum.

The finance is provided in May. None of the invoices was paid in May or June, but $200,000 was paid in July and $200,000 was paid in August.

Analysis

The discounter would provide $300,000 (75% of $400,000) to Delta in May. At the end of July, Delta would receive $50,000 (25% of $200,000) less charges, for the payments by customers in the month. Similarly, at the end of August, Delta would receive the remaining $50,000 (less charges).

Administration charges for invoice discounting are usually between 0.2% and 0.7% of turnover. There is an element of credit protection in an invoice discounting service, but its real purpose is to improve the client's cash flow. Because the invoice discounter does not control debt administration, and relies on the client to collect the debts, it is a more risky operation than factoring proper and a discounter will agree to offer a service only to reliable companies. A company that uses discounting finance usually will be operating credit terms of no more than 90 days and will have a turnover of at least $1 million per annum.

Invoice discounting could be suitable for larger companies wanting finance secured against the value of invoices but wishing to maintain control over the administration of invoices and debt collection, because they have a sophisticated sales administration system of their own.

Summary

Factoring can assist companies with their management of debtors, credit risk and cash flow. It can offer efficient sales administration, a credit control system based on a large data bank of credit information, and credit protection for approved debts.

A company could decide that the cost of a factoring service is justified by quicker debt collection and, quite possibly, fewer bad debts.

There should be on-going dialogue between the factor and the company to allow flexibility to increase limits to meet market needs.

Conclusion

This book has provided a framework for credit risk management. It has explained the nature of credit risk, as well as its potential cost, and has stressed the importance of credit control in containing the risk. Some risk is unavoidable, because credit must be granted to make more profits. Therefore a balance must be achieved between risk and return, particularly on marginal business.

Although specific procedures and methods for controlling risk differ between banks and other companies, the basic principles and approach to credit risk management are common to all types of company. There are two broad aspects to consider

- the management and control of credit (debtors), and
- where there could be doubts about the customer's ability to pay on time, the need for additional security.

The management and control of debtors requires a credit policy, a system for making individual credit decisions, an efficient organization, and operational procedures and systems for monitoring customer payments and control reporting.

Banks can ask for security, guarantees or loan covenants when there are doubts about the customer's ability to pay. Companies can seek comparable security of payment by different methods, such as payments in advance, letters of credit and credit insurance.

The concerns of credit risk management could be summarized, perhaps, by three questions. What is the credit risk for the company? How costly is the potential risk? Are suitable measures being taken to control and minimize the risk consistent with the company's requirement to win business and make profits?

Appendix

Presentation of Documents after Shipping

The checking of documents after shipment by the advising bank or issuing bank, is a crucial process. It is common for a bank to find errors.

The bank checks the documents that have been presented against the specifications in the letter of credit, to ensure that

- all the documents, as specified in the letter of credit, have been presented
- they are correct as to number, type and content
- they conform exactly to the requirements of the letter of credit
- they are consistent with one another
- they can be identified as relating to the same goods by means of corresponding package numbers or shipping marks
- they have been presented within the time stipulated by the letter of credit, and within the period of validity of the letter of credit. For example, the letter of credit may state that the documents should be presented within seven days of issuance of the bill of lading, and that the availability of the credit expires on January 31, 2002
- the insurance documents are correct.

A large proportion of letters of credit are invalidated because the beneficiary fails to present error-free documents on time to the named bank. The bank has an obligation to reject the documents even for a small error.

If there are any discrepancies, the documents are returned to the exporter (beneficiary) without payment. The discrepancies should be corrected if possible, but must be presented again within the time limit specified in the letter of credit. The bank could decide to make a payment in spite of a discrepancy, but would do so only against an indemnity. This means that if the buyer subsequently refuses to allow the discrepancy, the exporter must reimburse the paying bank.

Typical discrepancies banks find in checking documents are

- the letter of credit has expired, perhaps because of late shipment of the goods
- the documents have been presented after the period stipulated in the letter of credit
- the bill of lading or other transport document is not clean. This means that it contains a clause stating that the goods or packaging are in a defective condition
- the bill of lading is not marked freight paid when the letter of credit calls for CIF (cost, insurance and freight), or C & F (cost and freight) shipment terms. These terms call for freight charges to be paid by the supplier
- the goods are being shipped between different ports from those stated in the letter of credit
- the insurance risks covered are not those required by the letter of credit
- the insurance document presented is not the type required by the letter of credit, e.g. an insurance cover note or certificate might be presented when the letter of credit calls for an insurance policy document
- the shipment is under-insured
- the amount insured is in a different currency from the one stated in the letter of credit
- the description of the goods on the invoice differs from the description of the goods on the letter of credit
- the weight of the goods differs from one document to another
- the amount on the invoice differs from the amount on the bill of exchange
- the bill of exchange has been drawn on the wrong party.

Glossary

Aged Debtors' List
A report analyzing and quantifying overdue debts.

Asset Conversion Loan
Short-term loan to finance temporary, e.g. seasonal, build-up in working capital.

Bad Debt
An overdue debt that is judged uncollectable.

Bank Credit
Credit granted by a bank to a customer.

Basle Agreement (BIS rules)
International agreement specifying minimum capital adequacy requirements for banks.

Charge
Form of security giving a lending bank a prior claim over other creditors to payment of its debt out of the charged assets, in the event of default on loan repayments by the borrower. A charge can be a fixed charge on a specific asset or a floating charge on a class of assets, e.g. stocks and debtors.

Collection Cycle
Sequence of events from issuing an invoice to receipt of payment.

Confirmed Letter of Credit
Letter of credit in which a conditional guarantee of payment is given by a second, confirming bank, as well as the bank issuing the letter of credit.

Counterparty Risk
The risk that the other party to a transaction will fail to honor the contract terms.

Covenant
Written undertaking by a borrower to comply with a certain condition of lending. Breach of a lending covenant is an event of default, giving the bank a right of action against the borrower.

Credit Cycle
Sequence of events from the time a customer places an order to the time that payment is received.

Credit Risk
The risk of loss through non-payment or late payment of money owed.

Credit Scoring
System of categorizing creditworthiness by awarding points according to certain key features of a business, to produce a total credit score.

Credit-taken Ratio
A ratio comparing the amount currently owed by a customer and the annual sales turnover on the customer's account. A high ratio indicates a high credit risk.

Credit Utilization
The extent to which customers are using existing credit facilities, measured by current debts outstanding as a percentage of the credit limit.

Days' Sales Outstanding (DSO)
The average number of days a company is taking to collect its debts.

Documentary Credit
See Letter of Credit.

EDI (electronic data interchange)
Method of transmitting messages electronically. EDI can be used, for example, to send out invoices.

Event of Default
Breach of loan covenant by a borrower.

Evergreen Loan
Short-term loan to finance working capital that is continuously rolled over, and is, in effect, long-term lending.

Factor
A company that manages and finances trade debts on behalf of client companies. Factoring services are sale administration, credit protection and providing finance to the client against the security of approved invoices. Also called a Debt Factor.

Fixed Charge
See Charge.

Floating Charge
See Charge.

Forfaiting
A method of obtaining finance from a forfaiting bank, for the export of capital goods whereby the buyer obtains medium-term credit over several years.

Invoice Discounting
The purchase of selected invoices, i.e. trade debts, at a discount. An invoice discounter provides finance to a client by purchasing debts, and the discount reflects a rate of interest on the money advanced.

Letter of Credit
A method of payment for export sales, to which internationally agreed procedures can be applied, in which either one or two banks give a conditional guarantee of payment to a supplier on behalf of a buyer.

Lien
A form a security, giving a bank the right to retain certain property of a borrower until the debt is repaid.

Operational Cash Flow
Cash flow from the trading operations of a business, usually expressed as a net amount, i.e. cash inflows from customer payments minus payments for operating requirements.

Order Cycle
Sequence of events from the receiving of an order to dispatching goods or providing service, and issuing the invoice.

Pledge
A deposit with a bank of goods, negotiable instruments or documents of title to goods, as security for an advance.

Promissory Note
A promise to pay a stated amount of money on a specified date.

Retention of Title Clause
Clause in a sales contract whereby the supplier retains legal title to the goods until after the customer has paid for them.

Swap
An agreement between two parties to exchange a series of future payments. In an interest-rate coupon swap, the parties swap fixed for floating rate payments.

Trade Credit
Credit granted by a supplier to a customer.

UCP
Uniform Customs and Practice for Documentary Credits, an internationally agreed set of procedures for payment by letter of credit.

Value Chain
Stages of production and supply within an industry, from raw material production to sale of the final product to the end-consumer. Also called the supply chain.

Index

1394190

Howll